JAMESTOWN LITERATURE PROGRAM
Growth in Comprehension & Appreciation

Reading & Understanding

Poems

LEVEL I

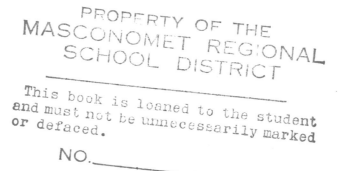

About the Cover and the Artist

The design on the cover of this book is a quilt called Contained Crazy Quilt, *created by internationally known quilt artist Jan Myers of Minneapolis, Minnesota. Jan is represented in many corporate and private collections, and in the permanent textiles collection of the Minneapolis Institute of Arts.*

Books in the Program

Short Stories, Level I
    Hardcover Edition
    Teacher's Guide

Nonfiction, Level I
    Hardcover Edition
    Teacher's Guide

Plays, Level I
    Hardcover Edition
    Teacher's Guide

Poems, Level I
    Hardcover Edition
    Teacher's Guide

Short Stories, Level II
    Hardcover Edition
    Teacher's Guide

Nonfiction, Level II
    Hardcover Edition
    Teacher's Guide

Plays, Level II
    Hardcover Edition
    Teacher's Guide

Poems, Level II
    Hardcover Edition
    Teacher's Guide

JAMESTOWN LITERATURE PROGRAM
Growth in Comprehension & Appreciation

Reading & Understanding
Poems

LEVEL I

JAMESTOWN PUBLISHERS

a division of NTC/CONTEMPORARY PUBLISHING GROUP
Lincolnwood, Illinois USA

JAMESTOWN LITERATURE PROGRAM
Growth in Comprehension & Appreciation

Reading & Understanding Poems
LEVEL I

Developed by Jamestown Editorial Group
and Helena Frost Associates, Gaynor Ellis, Editor

Cover and text design: Deborah Hulsey Christie
Photo Research: Helena Frost Associates

Illustrations:
    Chapters 2, 8, 9, 10, Jan Naimo Jones
    Chapter 6, Sandra Speidel
    Chapters 11, 12, Tom Sperling

Photographs:
Chapter 1, gold rush: The Bettmann Archive
Chapter 3, raven: Robert C. Hermes/Photo Researchers, Inc.
Chapter 3, Athena: Art Resource, Inc.
Chapter 4, Black Hawk's statue: Illinois State Historical Library
Chapter 4, daffodils: H. Armstrong Roberts
Chapter 5, Martin Luther King, Jr.: AP/Wide World Photos
Chapter 7, shoe factory: AP/Wide World Photos
Chapter 8, scene from Gettysburg: Ronald R. Thomas/Taurus Photos
Chapter 8, waves crashing on rocks: Terry Quinn/Frost Publishing Group

ISBN: 0-89061-692-2 (hardbound)
ISBN: 0-89061-489-X (softbound)

Published by Jamestown Publishers,
a division of NTC/Contemporary Publishing Group, Inc.,
4255 West Touhy Avenue,
Lincolnwood (Chicago), Illinois 60646-1975 U.S.A.

9 0 QB(H)) 10 9 8 7 6 5 4

Acknowledgments

Acknowledgment is gratefully made to the following individuals and publishers for permission to reprint the poems in this book.

"The Cremation of Sam McGee" by Robert Service. From *The Collected Poems of Robert Service.* Reprinted by permission of Dodd, Mead & Company.

"The Play" by David Wagoner. From *Through the Forest: New and Selected Poems, 1977–1987* by David Wagoner. Copyright © 1987 by David Wagoner. Reprinted by permission of The Atlantic Monthly Press. Originally appeared in *Poetry,* May 1985, published by The Modern Poetry Association; reprinted by permission of the editor of *Poetry.*

"View of a Lake" by William Carlos Williams. From *Collected Earlier Poems* by William Carlos Williams. Copyright © by New Directions Publishing Corporation.

"Illinois: At Night, Black Hawk's Statue Broods" by J. W. Rivers. Copyright © 1986 by The Modern Poetry Association. Reprinted by permission of the editor of *Poetry.*

"Not Seeing Is Believing" by Paul Petrie. First published in *The Treasury of American Poetry,* edited by Nancy Sullivan, Doubleday & Company Inc., 1978 and reprinted in *Not Seeing Is Believing,* Juniper Press, 1983, and *The Runners,* Slow Loris Press, 1986. Reprinted by permission of the author.

"Dream Deferred" by Langston Hughes. Copyright © 1951 by Langston Hughes. Reprinted from *The Panther and the Lash* by Langston Hughes. Reprinted by permission of Alfred A. Knopf, Inc.

"Martin Luther King Jr." by Gwendolyn Brooks. Reprinted by permission of Broadside Press.

"The Noise That Time Makes" by Merrill Moore. Reprinted by permission of Anne Leslie Moore.

"Factory Work" by Deborah Boe. Copyright © 1986 by The Modern Poetry Association. Reprinted by permission of the editor of *Poetry*.

"The River Merchant's Wife: A Letter" by Ezra Pound. From *Personae* by Ezra Pound. Copyright © 1926 by Ezra Pound. Reprinted by permission of New Directions Publishing Corporation.

"The Eagle That Is Forgotten" by Vachel Lindsay. From *Collected Poems* by Vachel Lindsay. Copyright © 1923 by Macmillan Publishing Company; copyright renewed © 1951 by Elizabeth C. Lindsay. Reprinted by permission of Macmillan Publishing Company.

"Grass" by Carl Sandburg. From *Cornhuskers* by Carl Sandburg. Copyright © 1918 by Holt, Rinehart and Winston, Inc; copyright renewed © 1946 by Carl Sandburg. Reprinted by permission of Harcourt Brace Jovanovich, Inc.

"A Deserted Barn" by Larry Woiwode. From *Beyond the Bedroom Wall* by Larry Woiwode. Copyright © 1965, 1966, 1967, 1968, 1969, 1970, 1971, 1972, 1973, 1974, 1975 by Larry Woiwode. Originally appeared in *The New Yorker*. Reprinted by permission of Farrar, Straus, & Giroux, Inc.

"Two Friends" by David Ignatow. From *Figures of the Human* by David Ignatow. Copyright © 1983 by David Ignatow. Reprinted by permission of Wesleyan University Press.

"Reason" by Josephine Miles. Reprinted by permission of Richard B. Miles, executor of the estate of Josephine Miles.

"Stopping by Woods on a Snowy Evening" by Robert Frost. From *The Poetry of Robert Frost*, edited by Edward Connery Latham. Copyright © 1923, 1969 by Holt, Rinehart and Winston. Copyright © 1951 by Robert Frost. Reprinted by permission of Henry Holt & Company.

"Cloud, Castle, Lake" by Lawrence Raab. Copyright © 1986 by The Modern Poetry Association. Reprinted by permission of the editor of *Poetry*.

Contents

To the Student

As a little child, you probably heard plenty of poetry, without realizing that it *was* poetry. You heard a particular kind of poetry called nursery rhymes. Some of them, such as "Three Blind Mice" and "The Itsy, Bitsy Spider," were songs. Because of those early experiences with poetry, many people think of poems as rhyming stories. That is one kind of poetry, but as you will learn in this book, there are many other kinds.

Poems can be written about any subject, just as stories can. Many poems have a deeper meaning behind their surface meaning. In such poems the obvious subject may symbolize, or stand for, another subject. Much of the pleasure of reading poetry comes from finding the clues that unlock those other meanings. You can discover those clues by learning the special language of poetry.

Poetry is written in a language of rhythms and images laid out in lines and stanzas rather than in sentences and paragraphs. Poems have a reputation for being difficult to understand because many people have not learned the special language used to discuss poetry. In this book you will learn about the language of poetry, much as you might learn a secret code. Once you break the code, you'll be able to understand and enjoy many kinds of poetry.

Each chapter in this book contains one or more poems and a lesson that teaches skills that will help you to interpret the poems. Those skills will also help you to get the most out of poems you read on your own in the future. Each chapter begins with an introduction to the story, to the poems, and to the poet or poets. Often, knowing a poet's background helps you to better understand his or her work. As you read, you will find several literary terms underlined in each chapter. The first time a term appears in the text, it is underlined and defined. In the glossary at the back of the book, a page reference following each term indicates where the term first appears.

Hearing
Poetry

*I*n Unit One you will begin to study poetry by looking at some basic characteristics of poems. What is it about a poem that makes it different from other forms of writing? On a printed page, a poem *looks* different from other kinds of writing. More important, when you read poetry aloud, it *sounds* different. What accounts for those differences? In short, what is a poem? That is the question you will examine in Chapter 1.

One feature common to almost all poems is their arrangement into lines. In prose writing line length is unimportant. Unless the sentence ends a paragraph, the words in a sentence continue across one line until the line is full. Then a new line begins. That is not the case in poetry, where the writer—the poet—decides where each line begins and ends. Why do poets break their lines in certain ways? What difference does it make? In Chapter 2 you will look at the various effects of the arrangement of lines in poetry.

Another characteristic of poetry is that the poet pays a great deal of attention to the sounds of words and phrases. When the end sounds of two or more words are the same, they are said to rhyme. Rhyme is a feature of many kinds of poetry, and rhyme can be used in a variety of ways. Some people think of rhyming and poetry as one and the same thing. They are not. Rhyme, like every other characteristic of poetry, is found in some poems and not in others. Nor is it the only sound effect that you will find in poetry. In Chapter 3 you will take a closer look not simply at rhyme but also at some other ways in which poets use sound.

The poems in Unit One, as well as those in the other units of this book, represent a wide variety of poetry. Poetry is told in a different way from a prose story. Identifying the differences between poetry and prose helps you to understand and appreciate the main characteristics of poetry.

Chapter 1

Selection   *The Cremation of Sam McGee*
                        ROBERT SERVICE

Lesson   *What Is a Poem?*

❖

About the Selection

Robert Service's poem "The Cremation of Sam McGee" is set in the Yukon Territory of northwestern Canada during the great gold rush. (The word *cremation* means the burning to ashes of a dead body.) In 1896 gold was discovered in the valley of the Klondike River. That discovery brought a surge of people to the Yukon.

By 1898 more than thirty thousand people had invaded the Yukon, an area that previously had been home to just a few hundred. The newcomers, who hoped to make a quick fortune in the gold fields, included miners and adventurers from all over the world.

The Yukon Territory is located next to Alaska. In this cold Arctic region, the summer sun melts only the top layer of the frozen soil. At the height of the short summers, the sun never sinks below the horizon, giving Arctic regions the name "land of the midnight sun."

For a few months in summer, the rivers are free of ice. During the gold rush, steamboats made the long journey up the rivers from the sea to supply the Yukon miners. These supply boats were in danger of being trapped by the ice, however, if they did not return to the sea before the onset of winter. As you will read, one such boat plays a part in "The Cremation of Sam McGee."

Yukon winters are long and bitter cold. For months everything, including the rivers and lakes, is frozen solid. The days are short, and the nights are long. During the daytime, the sun barely peeks over the horizon, and it appears for only a few hours each day. On occasion, the long nights are brightened by bands of many-colored lights known as the aurora borealis, or the northern lights. More often, the clear, cold, dreary nights are lit only by the moon and the stars.

At the time of the Yukon gold rush, the only form of transportation through this darkness and bitter cold was the dogsled. Miners loaded their long sleds with supplies and set their teams of huskies to work. Because miners often traveled alone, their dog teams were important to their survival.

In "The Cremation of Sam McGee" the <u>speaker</u>—the person or voice who is telling the story or that talks in the poem—is on his own. He is determined to keep a promise he made to his friend. In the wild northern climate, his mission grows into a strange fantasy. The climate and the darkness contribute to the fantasy.

Perhaps you have had an experience in which the seasons or the time of day affected your state of mind. For example, have you ever noticed that a walk on a warm summer's day seems far different from one on a bitter cold winter's night? How do the temperature and the time of day affect the atmosphere? Why does the dark winter walk seem more threatening?

Much of Robert Service's poetry reflects the influence of local stories and tales. He was born in England in 1874 and emigrated to Canada as a young man. Service spent his first few years in Canada working for a large bank. In 1904 the bank transferred him to the Yukon. There he found the setting that would inspire his poems, novels, and articles.

Many of Service's poems take the form of dramatic monologues— a single person, not necessarily the poet, is speaking directly to a listener, even if only to himself or herself. In "The Cremation of Sam McGee" the speaker is a character who participates in the events of the poem.

During his lifetime, Service's Yukon poetry was very popular. Profits from the publication of his poems enabled him to retire from his bank job and concentrate on writing. Service eventually moved to France, where he died in 1958.

"The Cremation of Sam McGee" is <u>narrative poetry</u>—a poem that tells a story. The story, however, is told in a different way from a prose story.

Lesson Preview

The lesson that follows "The Cremation of Sam McGee" focuses on what a poem is. How does a poem differ from other kinds of writing, such as a short story? If you ask people, "What makes a poem a poem?" they might answer, "I can't say exactly, but I know a poem when I see one." This answer suggests that a poem has some readily recognizable features. You will learn what those features are in the lesson.

"The Cremation of Sam McGee" tells an eerie story of life in the Yukon. Despite the bizarre events, you can't help smiling at the end of the story. Robert Service has chosen to tell this story in a poem rather than in a short story. The questions that follow will help you identify some features of the poem. As you read, think about how you would answer these questions.

1 You know as soon as you look at "The Cremation of Sam McGee" that it is a poem. How do you know this?

2 Look at how the poem is divided into sections, or parts. How do the sections compare to each other in length?

3 Read several parts of the poem out loud. What do you notice about the rhythm, or beat, of the poem? Is the rhythm the same in each line?

4 If Service had chosen to write about Sam McGee's cremation in a short story, do you think the story would have been longer or shorter than the poem. Why?

Vocabulary

Here are some difficult words that appear in the poem that follows. Study the words and their definitions, as well as the sentences that show how the words are used. This will help you get the most from your reading.

moil   work hard. *Because Sue has a difficult time understanding math concepts, she will often moil and toil over her homework for hours without understanding it at all.*

lashed fastened; tied. *The huge Christmas tree would not fit in the trunk so we lashed it to the roof of the car.*

brawn muscular strength. *Distressed by his lack of brawn, George decided to begin lifting weights.*

hearkened listened with attention. *The excited children stopped playing and hearkened to the distant sound of an ice cream truck.*

trice a moment; a brief space of time. *I only meant to close my eyes for a trice, but instead I fell asleep for several hours.*

grisly marked by a sense of grim horror. *The paramedics quickly arrived at the scene of the grisly automobile accident.*

The Cremation of Sam McGee

Robert Service

There are strange things done in the midnight sun
By the men who moil for gold;
The Arctic trails have their secret tales
That would make your blood run cold;
5 *The Northern Lights have seen queer sights,*
But the queerest they ever did see
Was that night on the marge¹ of Lake Lebarge
I cremated Sam McGee.

Now Sam McGee was from Tennessee, where the cotton blooms and
blows.
10 Why he left his home in the South to roam 'round the Pole, God only
knows.
He was always cold, but the land of gold seemed to hold him like a spell;
Though he'd often say in his homely way that "he'd sooner live in hell."

On a Christmas Day we were mushing our way over the Dawson trail.
Talk of your cold! through the parka's fold it stabbed like a driven nail.
15 If our eyes we'd close, then the lashes froze till sometimes we couldn't
see;
It wasn't much fun, but the only one to whimper was Sam McGee.

And that very night, as we lay packed tight in our robes beneath the snow,
And the dogs were fed, and the stars o'erhead were dancing heel and toe,
He turned to me, and "Cap," says he, "I'll cash in this trip, I guess;
20 And if I do, I'm asking that you won't refuse my last request."

Well, he seemed so low that I couldn't say no; then he says with a sort
of moan:

---

1. **marge:** edge.

What Is a Poem?

"It's the cursèd cold, and it's got right hold till I'm chilled clean through
    to the bone.
Yet 'tain't being dead—it's my awful dread of the icy grave that pains;
So I want you to swear that, foul or fair, you'll cremate my last remains."

25 A pal's last need is a thing to heed, so I swore I would not fail;
And we started on at the streak of dawn; but God! he looked ghastly pale.
He crouched on the sleigh, and he raved all day of his home in Tennessee;
And before nightfall a corpse was all that was left of Sam McGee.

There wasn't a breath in that land of death, and I hurried, horror-driven,
30 With a corpse half hid that I couldn't get rid, because of a promise given;
It was lashed to the sleigh, and it seemed to say: "You may tax your brawn
    and brains,
But you promised true, and it's up to you to cremate those last remains."

Now a promise made is a debt unpaid, and the trail has its own stern code.
In the days to come, though my lips were dumb, in my heart how I
    cursed that load.
35 In the long, long night, by the lone firelight, while the huskies, round in
    a ring,
Howled out their woes to the homeless snows—O God! how I loathed
    the thing.

And every day that quiet clay seemed to heavy and heavier grow;
And on I went, though the dogs were spent and the grub was getting low;
The trail was bad, and I felt half mad, but I swore I would not give in;
40 And I'd often sing to the hateful thing, and it hearkened with a grin.

Till I came to the marge of Lake Lebarge, and a derelict there lay;
It was jammed in the ice, but I saw in a trice it was called the "Alice May."
And I looked at it, and I thought a bit, and I looked at my frozen chum;
Then "Here," said I, with a sudden cry, "is my cre-ma-tor-eum."

45 Some planks I tore from the cabin floor, and I lit the boiler fire;
Some coal I found that was lying around, and I heaped the fuel higher;
The flames just soared, and the furnace roared—such a blaze you seldom see;
And I burrowed a hole in the glowing coal, and I stuffed in Sam McGee.

Then I made a hike, for I didn't like to hear him sizzle so;
50 And the heavens scowled, and the huskies howled, and the wind began to blow.
It was icy cold, but the hot sweat rolled down my cheeks, and I don't know why;
And the greasy smoke in an inky cloak went streaking down the sky.

I do not know how long in the snow I wrestled with grisly fear;
But the stars came out and they danced about ere again I ventured near;
55 I was sick with dread, but I bravely said: "I'll just take a peep inside.
I guess he's cooked, and it's time I looked"—then the door I opened wide.

And there sat Sam, looking cool and calm, in the heart of the furnace roar;
And he wore a smile you could see a mile, and he said: "Please close that door.
It's fine in here, but I greatly fear you'll let in the cold and storm—
60 Since I left Plumtree, down in Tennessee, it's the first time I've been warm."

There are strange things done in the midnight sun
  By the men who moil for gold;
The Arctic trails have their secret tales
  That would make your blood run cold;
65 The Northern Lights have seen queer sights,
  But the queerest they ever did see
Was the night on the marge of Lake Lebarge
  I cremated Sam McGee.

What Is a Poem?

Reviewing the Selection

Answer each of the following questions. You may look back at the poem if necessary.

Recalling Facts

1. Sam McGee died on
   - ☐ a. his birthday.
   - ☐ b. Groundhog Day.
   - ☐ c. the Fourth of July.
   - ☐ d. the day after Christmas.

Understanding Main Ideas

2. Why did Sam McGee want his body to be cremated?
   - ☐ a. It was required by law.
   - ☐ b. He hated the cold so much that he did not want his body to stay frozen.
   - ☐ c. He wanted his ashes taken home to Tennessee because his family was there.
   - ☐ d. The dead in his family had always been cremated.

Placing Events in Order

3. When did McGee rave "all day of his home in Tennessee"?
   - ☐ a. when he was cremated
   - ☐ b. every day
   - ☐ c. just before he died
   - ☐ d. in the nightmare of the person telling the story

Finding Supporting Details

4. What does the speaker do that shows he "felt half mad"?
   - ☐ a. He burrows a hole in the ice.
   - ☐ b. He sees the northern lights.
   - ☐ c. He sings to the frozen corpse.
   - ☐ d. He wrestles with a grizzly bear.

5. "Till I came to the marge of Lake Lebarge, and
   a <u>derelict</u> there lay." In this context *derelict*
   means
   ☐ a. an abandoned ship.
   ☐ b. a pile of wood.
   ☐ c. a tramp.
   ☐ d. a railroad station.

Interpreting the Selection

Answer each of the following questions. You may look back at the poem
if necessary.

6. What can you infer from the words "the
   flames just soared, and the furnace roared"?
   ☐ a. The fire needed more fuel.
   ☐ b. The fire was very large and hot.
   ☐ c. The fire was hard to start.
   ☐ d. The fire was out of control.

7. According to the evidence in the poem,
   the Yukon
   ☐ a. can be a dangerous place.
   ☐ b. makes people greedy.
   ☐ c. has a relatively mild climate.
   ☐ d. has helped many men get rich.

What Is a Poem?

8. The author's purpose in writing this poem is
   - ☐ a. to tell a ghostly story.
   - ☐ b. to tell a story about the Yukon.
   - ☐ c. to entertain the reader.
   - ☐ d. all of the above.

9. An important difference between this poem and a short story is the
   - ☐ a. way the lines are organized.
   - ☐ b. kinds of characters in the poem.
   - ☐ c. setting in the Arctic.
   - ☐ d. story that is told.

10. The speaker agreed to cremate Sam McGee because
    - ☐ a. both Sam and he came from Tennessee.
    - ☐ b. Sam had once saved his life.
    - ☐ c. Sam had left all his goods to the speaker.
    - ☐ d. Sam was his pal.

What Is a Poem?

When people speak or write, they usually do so in prose. <u>Prose</u> is the ordinary form of written or spoken language, without any rhyme or regular rhythm. It is the language of our everyday activities. It is the language of everyday speech and ordinary conversation. Prose is also the language of much literature. Novels, short stories, essays, and many plays are written in prose.

What, then, is poetry? Poetry has many elements. However, because poems vary a great deal, you will not find all the elements of poetry in every poem. Traditionally, <u>poetry</u> is defined as a type of literature in which the rhythm, sound, and meaning of language are arranged to create powerful images and feelings. Poetry is arranged in lines with a regular rhythm and sometimes a pattern of rhyme. Some poems, however, do not have a regular rhythm or rhyme.

In this lesson you will study four major elements found in many poems: the arrangement of lines, the division of lines into stanzas, the regular rhythm and meter, and the compactness of the language. Poetry has many other elements that you will learn about in later chapters.

Arrangement of Lines

As soon as you look at "The Cremation of Sam McGee," you know it is a poem. Why? The most obvious feature is its arrangement into separate lines rather than into sentences that run together. Lines of poetry may be long or short, depending on where the poet wants you to pause. Poets often vary the lengths of lines in order to emphasize certain ideas. The arrangement of lines in poetry affects the way you read and understand the words.

Look, for example, at lines 5 to 8 of the poem:

> The Northern Lights have seen queer sights,
> But the queerest they ever did see
> Was that night on the marge of Lake Lebarge
> I cremated Sam McGee.

Compare those lines with this sentence:

> The Northern Lights have seen queer sights, but the queerest they ever did see was that night on the marge of Lake Lebarge I cremated Sam McGee.

Both versions have the same words and the same punctuation. The only differences are that in the second version the lines have been run together and a few capital letters have been changed to lowercase. Yet if you compare the poetry lines to the sentence, the effect is quite different.

The reason for the difference lies in the arrangement of the poem. It causes you to pause slightly at the end of each line. You do not do that when the same words are written as a sentence. In the poem the pauses make you emphasize the last word of each line. They force you to read in a regular rhythm. It is almost as if the poet had underlined certain words or written them in capital letters, as shown here:

> The Northern Lights have seen queer SIGHTS,
> But the queerest they ever did SEE
> Was that night on the marge of Lake LEBARGE
> I cremated Sam McGEE.

You can see how this emphasis works by taking any ordinary sentence and arranging it in lines like a poem. Look at the following examples:

Examples:	You can see how	You can see how this emphasis
	this emphasis works	works by taking
	by taking any	any
	ordinary sentence	ordinary
	and arranging	sentence
	it in lines	and arranging it in lines
	like a poem.	like a poem.

1. Find a sentence in a textbook and arrange it into a four- or five-line poem. Read the original sentence and then your sentence-poem aloud. How do they differ?

Division of Lines into Stanzas

A distinguishing feature of many poems is their division into stanzas. A stanza is a group of lines that forms a section of a poem. Each stanza usually has the same rhyme pattern.

The poet indicates the end of one stanza and the beginning of another by leaving a space between them. Of course, not every poem is divided into stanzas. In many poems the stanzas have a fixed pattern. Each stanza may have the same number of lines, and the same rhyme pattern.

2. Look at "The Cremation of Sam McGee." How many stanzas does the poem have? Notice that all but two of the stanzas have the same number of lines. How many lines are there in most of the stanzas?

The two stanzas that are different appear at the beginning and end of the poem. They are unlike the rest of the poem in several ways. First, they are printed in italics, or slanted type, to set them apart from the rest of the poem. Second, the lines are shorter than those in the rest of the poem. Third, the two stanzas are almost identical.

3. Look at the first and last stanzas. How are they different? What purpose do you think they serve in "The Cremation of Sam McGee"?

Rhythm and Meter

Stress. In both poetry and prose, some words or syllables receive greater stress, or accent, than others. Sometimes, words or syllables are stressed because of where they are placed in a phrase or because of the natural speech patterns of a language. At other times, a word is stressed because of its pronunciation.

Poets take advantage of natural speech patterns and the pronunciation of words to emphasize certain stressed syllables. Sometimes they write lines in such a way as to emphasize a word or syllable that you might not ordinarily stress. Notice, for example, the stressed syllables in the first lines of "The Cremation of Sam McGee."

> There are STRANGE things DONE in the MIDnight SUN
> By the MEN who MOIL for GOLD;

The words or syllables in capital letters are said to be accented, or stressed. The other words are unaccented, or unstressed.

Robert Service has chosen his words and arranged them in such a way that certain words and syllables are stressed. For example, the first line begins with two rather dull, passive words—"there" and "are." They point the way to a third word, *strange,* that carries an emotional message. Notice how the poet builds up to each of the other stressed words or syllables in the succeeding lines.

Rhythm. The pattern of stressed and unstressed syllables is called rhythm. Through rhythm, poets can highlight the musical quality of language. Rhythm can serve other purposes, too, such as emphasizing ideas or making actions more vivid.

The standard way of showing the rhythm of a poem is by using this symbol, ╱ , for a stressed syllable, and this one, ◡, for an unstressed syllable. Thus, the rhythm of the first two lines of "The Cremation of Sam McGee" can be illustrated like this:

> ◡ ◡ ╱ ◡ ╱ ◡ ◡ ╱ ◡ ╱
> There are strange things done in the midnight sun
> ◡ ◡ ╱ ◡ ╱ ◡ ╱
> By the men who moil for gold;

4. Copy a stanza from the poem and mark each line to show the stressed and unstressed syllables.

Meter. Did you notice that the rhythm of the lines you copied has a regular pattern? In some poems the rhythm changes from line to line or even within lines. In others the rhythm is regular. "The Cremation of Sam McGee" has a regular rhythmic pattern. The regular pattern of stressed and unstressed syllables in a line of poetry is called <u>meter</u>.

You can discover the meter of a poem by <u>scanning</u>, or counting, the number and arrangement of stressed (strong) and unstressed (weak) syllables in a line. Meter is counted in units called feet. A <u>foot</u> usually consists of one stressed syllable and its one or more unstressed syllables. The number of feet in a line of poetry is counted by the number of stressed syllables. Repeat the following line several times. Try saying the unstressed syllables very softly and saying the stressed syllables with more force.

> ⌣ ⌣ ／⌣ ／ ⌣ ⌣ ／ ⌣ ／ ⌣ ⌣
> And that very night, as we lay packed tight in our
> ／ ⌣ ／ ⌣ ／
> robes beneath the snow,

Scan the lines of the stanza that you copied and marked earlier. Notice that the number of feet per line varies.

Even when the meter of a poem appears to be regular, you may be in for an occasional surprise. When poets want to draw attention to certain words, they may break the pattern. The word that breaks the pattern then stands out. Scan the first three stanzas. Then look closely at line 14.

> ／ ⌣ ⌣ ／ ⌣ ⌣ ／⌣ ／⌣ ／ ⌣ ⌣
> Talk of your cold! through the parka's fold it stabbed like a
> ／ ⌣ ／
> driven nail.

Every other line in the first three stanzas begins with one or two unstressed syllables. In this line, however, the word *talk* breaks the pattern. It receives greater emphasis in the line and actually stands out in the stanza.

5. Scan the last two lines of the first stanza. How does the poet break the pattern in those lines? What word is emphasized as a result?

What Is a Poem?

Compactness of Language

Compared to other kinds of literature, poetry is very compact. Poetry is concentrated and generally uses fewer words than prose to achieve its purposes. Poets usually give you fewer details and less explanation than prose writers do. Instead, poets use words to create pictures or to appeal to the senses.

In "The Cremation of Sam McGee" Robert Service tells you that Sam and Cap were "mushing" their way over the Dawson trail on a Christmas Day, but he does not say what they were doing there. In a prose story the writer would probably explain why they were traveling on that day. Similarly, when Sam tells Cap, "I'll cash in this trip, I guess," you don't know whether Sam has been ill for a long time or whether he was simply overcome by the cold on that trip.

Look at Cap's reason for agreeing to Sam's last wish. It is a compact, or tight, statement: "A pal's last need is a thing to heed, so I swore I would not fail." That brief statement tells you a lot about Cap's idea of friendship and the kind of person he is. It does not, however, tell you how long the two men have been friends or what the basis for their friendship was.

6. Reread stanzas 10 and 11, in which Cap describes finding the makeshift crematorium. Imagine that you are writing a short story about the incident described in the poem. Describe in your own words what happens in those stanzas. Then compare your prose to Service's poetry. How is the language similar? How is it different?

Narrative Poetry

You will be reading many types of poetry in this book. "The Cremation of Sam McGee" is a narrative poem. As you read in the introduction to this chapter, narrative poetry is poetry that tells a story. The story may be true or it may be imagined. The story in "The Cremation of Sam McGee" is undoubtedly fiction—an invention of the poet's imagination.

In many ways, this narrative poem is like a short story. It has a setting, a time and place in which the action takes place. It has characters, the people, animals, things, or machines that act or speak in the poem. It has a <u>plot</u>, or sequence of events.

The first stanza tells where and suggests when the narrative takes place. The setting is the Arctic, on the edge of Lake Lebarge. The events take place during the gold rush era.

7. What other details about the setting do you learn from the poem?

The poet introduces two characters: the speaker and Sam McGee. At one point, Sam calls the speaker "Cap."

8. What is the relationship between Sam and Cap? How can you tell?

The narrative reveals a series of strange events. In stanzas 3 to 6 Cap tells about the events leading to Sam's death and about his promise to Sam. In the next three stanzas Cap reveals his horror at being alone with the corpse. Then in stanzas 12 to 14 he describes the fire and the strange sight he saw. The poem builds to the <u>climax</u>, or the point of highest tension and greatest interest for you.

9. What is the climax in the poem? Why is it so intense?

The poem ends the way it began. Do you get the feeling that by repeating the opening stanza the speaker is suggesting that he could tell still more tales of strange and bizarre happenings in the Arctic?

Questions for Thought and Discussion

The questions and activities that follow will help you to explore "The Cremation of Sam McGee" in more depth and at the same time develop your critical thinking skills.

1. **Analyzing the Setting.** The setting is more important in some narrative poems than in others. How important is the setting in this poem? Support your answer with examples from the poem.

2. **Recognizing the Language of Poetry.** The first stanzas of the poem emphasize the Yukon's cold. The next few stanzas keep drawing your

attention to the corpse. Then several stanzas emphasize the great size and heat of the fire. In each case the poet describes the cold, the corpse, and the heat in a different way. Find three ways in the poem in which he refers to each.

3. **Predicting Outcomes.** The narrative stops very suddenly with Sam's last words. What do you suppose might have happened next? Discuss several possibilities. Do you think Service should have continued the poem? Explain your answer.

4. **Evaluating Character.** What kind of person do you think Sam McGee was? What kind of person is Cap, the speaker? Use details from the poem to support your view of each character.

Writing About Literature

Several suggestions for writing projects are given below. You may be asked to complete one or more of these projects. If you have any questions about how to begin a writing assignment, review Using the Writing Process, beginning on page 249.

1. **Summarizing.** A summary is a brief statement that tells the main points in a few words. Write a plot summary of "The Cremation of Sam McGee."

2. **Reporting on Research.** Find out about the climate of the Yukon in the summer and the winter. Then write a brief report describing the climate of the region and comparing it to the climate of the region in which you live.

3. **Writing a Narrative.** Think of a strange or unusual experience you or someone you know has had. Write a brief narrative describing the experience. You may write the story in prose or in poetry.

4. **Writing an Explanation.** Copy a stanza from "The Cremation of Sam McGee," marking each syllable in the stanza as stressed [∕] or unstressed [∪]. What kinds of words are stressed (adjectives, nouns, verbs)? What kinds of pictures or feelings do those words suggest?

Chapter 2

❖

About the Selections

In the first chapter, you read a narrative poem, "The Cremation of Sam McGee," and learned about some of the differences between poetry and prose. Poetry *looks* different from prose because it has a different arrangement of lines. In this chapter you will read three short poems and examine the various effects created by the arrangement of lines.

The three poems in this chapter vary in several ways. First, the poets lived at different times. Second, their subjects are very different. One talks about football, the second about a scene near a lake, and the third about the various stages in a man's life. Finally, the language, line lengths, and organization of the poems also differ.

Do you know what a defensive lineman does? The first poem, David Wagoner's "The Play," requires at least a little knowledge of football. The defensive lineman's job is to try to stop the opposing team from completing a play. The lineman is big but also fast. When the ball is snapped to the quarterback, the lineman rushes forward to stop the quarterback from passing. The poem gives a sense of power and action. Even though "The Play" is, on the surface, about football, it has other meanings as well.

The second poem is "View of a Lake" by William Carlos Williams. The poem is, as its title suggests, a description of a view of a lake. You don't know if the view is of an actual lake or of a lake that the poet has imagined. Williams does not name the lake, nor does he tell where it is.

The third poem, "The Seven Ages of Man," was written almost four hundred years ago. Its author, William Shakespeare, is recognized as one of the greatest poets and playwrights to have written in English. Although "The Seven Ages of Man" appears here as a separate poem, it is actually part of Shakespeare's play *As You Like It.* In the play, the lines are spoken by a character named Jaques (pronounced JAKE-is).

Jaques is a cynic—someone who believes that people are motivated by selfishness and who finds fault with others and their beliefs. In this poem Jaques says that one man's life is the same as another's. In other words, everyone's life follows the same pattern. Yet the poem says this in an original and amusing way.

Of the three poets, David Wagoner is the only one still living. He was born in Massillon, Ohio, in 1926. His first book of poems and his first novel were published when he was in his thirties. He has continued to publish both poetry and fiction while teaching at the University of Washington. Wagoner is recognized as a leading poet of his generation. Critics have praised his poems for their "sudden leaps . . . that dazzle, tease, and give pleasure."

William Carlos Williams, the author of "View of a Lake," was born in 1883 in Rutherford, New Jersey. After high school, Williams studied medicine. From 1909 on, he practiced medicine in his hometown, specializing in pediatrics—the care of children.

Williams continued to write poetry, as well as short stories, throughout his life. He also wrote his autobiography. Williams was influenced by the imagist movement of poetry. The movement stressed the importance of precisely presenting an image, not just describing the image. "View of a Lake" reflects this influence. Williams presents the scene with words almost as if it were a painting or a photograph.

Shakespeare's name is known worldwide. Even in his own day, his genius was recognized. Yet for a writer of such importance, surprisingly little is known about Shakespeare. It is known that he was born in 1564 in the small English town of Stratford-upon-Avon, and he probably lived there until he was in his twenties.

About 1590, Shakespeare joined a company of actors who performed plays in London. As far as anyone now knows, he was never a leading actor, but he quickly became the company's most successful playwright. Within about twenty years, he wrote at least thirty-seven plays. About 1613, he retired to Stratford, where he died in 1616.

Lesson Preview

The lesson that follows the three poems focuses on the structure of poetry, which is the poet's arrangement or overall design of the work. In poetry the structure refers to the way the words and lines are arranged to produce a particular effect. In the lesson you will examine how lines and stanzas can be arranged and the effects of various arrangements.

To understand how the arrangement of lines and stanzas affects a poem, skim each poem to find the punctuation that shows where sentences begin and end. The first time you read the poem, pause after each line to think about what the line means. Ask yourself, What is the poet saying? On your second time through, read the poem from beginning to end without stopping.

The questions that follow will help you study the structure of each poem. As you read, think about how you would answer these questions.

1 How does the line arrangement of "The Play" cause certain words to be emphasized? What words seem to receive the greatest emphasis?

2 "View of a Lake" has no periods, although there are other punctuation marks. How can you tell where one sentence ends and another begins? How does the lack of periods affect the way you read the poem?

3 What punctuation does "View of a Lake" use? Why do you think the poet uses the punctuation in the places you found it?

4 How do the lines in "The Seven Ages of Man" differ from those in the other two poems?

Vocabulary

Here are some difficult words that appear in Shakespeare's poem "The Seven Ages of Man." Study the words and their definitions, as well as the sentences that show how the words are used. This will help you get the most from your reading.

satchel a small bag for carrying clothes or books. *Sue decided to take a satchel of clothes home and to send for the rest of her belongings later.*

capon a rooster fattened for eating. *Because our family is small, we decided to have a capon for Thanksgiving rather than a large turkey.*

saws old sayings; proverbs. *We were tired of hearing our grandmother repeat the same old saws she had been quoting for years.*

instances examples. *The police department's report cited several instances of vandalism and theft in the neighborhood.*

shank the lower part of the leg. *The veterinarian carefully checked the horse's bruised shank for any signs of a more serious injury.*

treble a high-pitched voice. *The clear, pure treble of the boys' choir echoed throughout the cathedral.*

The Play

DAVID WAGONER

Crouching, he was falling
Forward suddenly the way
A lineman should go
At the snap from center:
5   Headlong but holding
His same position
Against all interference,
All trick shifts, his weight
Overbalanced heavily
10   Toward what came rushing
Against him, that carrier,
That wingback. We lifted him
Clumsily halfway under
The slump of the shoulders,
15   His shape so solid now,
So gray, we could hardly
Budge him. He thought
He had to be there
With his whole body
20   To defend his territory,
Arms locked so no one
Could get through
Without his say-so.
He was still
25   In the game, a part
Of the action, the team-player,
The loyal tackler, rock-sure
Through all those losing seasons

Believing he was the key
30 To every play though never
More than one more number
To the real play-maker.
Exit on a stretcher
The heavy father.

View of a Lake

WILLIAM CARLOS WILLIAMS

from a
highway below a face
of rock

too recently blasted
5 to be overgrown
with grass or fern:

Where a
waste of cinders
slopes down to

10 the railroad and
the lake
stand three children

beside the weed-grown
chassis
15 of a wrecked car

immobile in a line
facing the water
To the left a boy

in falling off
20 blue overalls
Next to him a girl

in a grimy frock
And another boy
They are intent

25 watching something
below—?
A section sign: 50

on an iron post
planted
30 by a narrow concrete

service hut
(to which runs
a sheaf of wires)

in the universal
35 cinders beaten
into crossing paths

to form the front yard
of a frame house
at the right

Structure: Lines and Stanzas

40 that looks
to have been flayed
Opposite

remains a sycamore
in leaf
45 Intently fixed

the three
with straight backs
ignore

the stalled traffic
50 all eyes
toward the water

The Seven Ages of Man

WILLIAM SHAKESPEARE

All the world's a stage,
And all the men and women merely players:
They have their exits and their entrances;
And one man in his time plays many parts,
5 His acts being seven ages. At first the infant,
Mewling[1] and puking in the nurse's arms.
And then the whining school-boy, with his satchel,
And shining morning face, creeping like snail
Unwillingly to school. And then the lover

1. **mewling:** crying weakly.

♦

10 Sighing like furnace, with a woeful ballad
Made to his mistress' eyebrow. Then a soldier,
Full of strange oaths, and bearded like the pard,[2]
Jealous in honour, sudden and quick in quarrel,
Seeking the bubble reputation
15 Even in the cannon's mouth. And then the justice,
In fair round belly with good capon lin'd,
With eyes severe, and beard of formal cut,
Full of wise saws and modern instances;
And so he plays his part. The sixth age shifts
20 Into the lean and slipper'd pantaloon,[3]
With spectacles on nose and pouch on side,
His youthful hose well sav'd a world too wide
For his shrunk shank; and his big manly voice,
Turning again toward childish treble, pipes
25 And whistles in his sound. Last scene of all,
That ends this strange eventful history,
Is second childishness and mere oblivion,
Sans[4] teeth, sans eyes, sans taste, sans everything.

2. pard: leopard. **3. pantaloon:** a character in popular plays of the time, portrayed as an old man in slippers and tight trousers. **4. sans:** a French word meaning without.

Reviewing the Selections

Answer each of the following questions. You may look back at the poems if necessary.

Recalling Facts

1. In "The Seven Ages of Man" the poet says that all people are like
   ☐ a. poets.
   ☐ b. actors on a stage.
   ☐ c. flowers.
   ☐ d. acrobats in a circus.

Understanding Main Ideas

2. "The Play" has to do with a play in a
   ☐ a. theater.
   ☐ b. large corporation.
   ☐ c. school auditorium.
   ☐ d. football game.

Placing Events in Order

3. In "The Seven Ages of Man" the "soldier, full of strange oaths," comes just after the
   ☐ a. "lover sighing like furnace."
   ☐ b. "whining school-boy."
   ☐ c. "justice, in fair round belly."
   ☐ d. "infant, mewling and puking."

Finding Supporting Details

4. In "View of a Lake" what are the children watching?
   ☐ a. They are watching the stalled traffic on the highway.
   ☐ b. They are stopping to look at the wrecked car.
   ☐ c. They are watching a passing railroad train.
   ☐ d. The poem does not say what they are watching.

5. "Where a / waste of cinders / slopes down to / the railroad and / the lake / stand three children / beside the weed-grown / chassis / of a wrecked car / <u>immobile</u> in a line / facing the water." In this context *immobile* means
   ☐ a. not moving.
   ☐ b. playing a game.
   ☐ c. waving.
   ☐ d. lying down.

Interpreting the Selections

Answer each of the following questions. You may look back at the poems if necessary.

6. In "The Play" the phrase "the real play-maker" might refer to
   ☐ a. death.
   ☐ b. God.
   ☐ c. the football coach.
   ☐ d. any of the above.

7. Read the first and last stanzas of "View of a Lake." From those stanzas you can conclude that the person who is viewing the lake is
   ☐ a. in a car held up in traffic on the highway.
   ☐ b. in a boat on the lake.
   ☐ c. looking out the window of the frame house.
   ☐ d. sitting at the edge of the lake.

8. Which poem helps you find meaning in the details of everyday life?
   - ☐ a. "View of a Lake"
   - ☐ b. "The Play"
   - ☐ c. "The Seven Ages of Man"
   - ☐ d. all three poems

9. Read aloud the first few lines of each poem. Which poem has a more definite meter than the others?
   - ☐ a. "The Play"
   - ☐ b. "View of a Lake"
   - ☐ c. "The Seven Ages of Man"
   - ☐ d. All three have a similar meter.

10. The lake in "View of a Lake" is probably
    - ☐ a. in the Rocky Mountains.
    - ☐ b. in or near a city.
    - ☐ c. surrounded by summer resorts.
    - ☐ d. in Mexico.

Structure: Lines and Stanzas

Structure is the way in which a piece of literature is put together. In poems structure refers to the way the words and lines are arranged to produce a particular effect. In this lesson you will examine how the lines are arranged in each of the three poems you just read and the effect each arrangement has on the poem. By looking at the different ways in which poets can arrange lines and breaks in their works, you can begin to see the great variety in poetry.

At first glance some poems look hard to read or understand. Until people learn *how* to read poetry, they are often more comfortable reading prose. Once you understand the structure of a poem, however, you can begin to appreciate its other qualities.

Line Arrangement in "The Play"

A good way to read a poem for the first time is to look at it as though it were made up of ordinary sentences. That method of reading a poem helps you to understand its basic idea. If you follow that advice for "The Play," you can read the first twelve lines in this way:

Crouching, he was falling forward suddenly the way a lineman should go at the snap from center: headlong but holding his same position against all interference, all trick shifts, his weight overbalanced heavily toward what came rushing against him, that carrier, that wingback.

When lines of poetry are run together, they make a complex sentence, which is often difficult to read. Even so, many people find it easier to read a long sentence like that than lines of poetry. The reason is that you are used to reading and speaking prose, which is written in sentences.

1. Rewrite the rest of the poem in ordinary sentences. Do you find it easier to read? Do you find it easier to understand the poem's meaning? Why or why not?

Identifying Who, What, Where. The purpose of reading the poem as though it were written in sentences is to understand its meaning better. Look again at the first sentence. It tells you that someone (the poet calls him "he") is "falling forward suddenly." The rest of the sentence gives details about his fall.

From the details, you begin to learn who is involved in "The Play," what he is doing, and where the poem is set. You realize that the poet is describing a football player in action on the field. In the second sentence, you learn that the football player has been injured. Some other people—other players, perhaps—are taking care of him.

2. Look at the remaining lines of "The Play" that you have written as sentences. After each sentence, explain what you think is happening. When you get to the last sentence, try to explain how it relates to the earlier sentences.

Levels of Meaning. Does the last sentence leave you wondering whether the poem is about something more than football? A poem can have different levels of meaning, or ways of being interpreted and understood. One level is based on the surface meaning, which focuses on the obvious or literal meaning of the words.

3. Look at lines 17 to 23. What is the surface meaning of those lines?

A deeper level of meaning is the symbolic meaning, in which the words stand for something else. A <u>symbol</u> is a person, a place, or an object that stands for something other or more important than itself. On a symbolic level, objects and actions are symbols for other objects or for ideas or qualities. The words suggest an image other than the one that is actually being described.

4. Reread the first four sentences of the poem. What else, besides football, might the poem be about? Write one or two possibilities.

Pauses and Emphasis. If you read "The Play" as it is written, you notice that the lines are very short. Each has between three and five words. Read a few lines aloud several times. Listen closely to how the words sound as you move from line to line. When you reach the end of each line, you probably find it natural to pause. That short pause makes you hold on to the last word of a line. It is as if those words were slowed down a bit. The pause makes the words more noticeable or more important.

The pause also affects the first word or two of the next line. After the pause, you press on, giving added emphasis to the first words of the new line.

5. Look at the first five lines of "The Play." Identify three or four words that get special emphasis from their position either at the end or the beginning of a line.

6. Reread lines 1 to 12. How do the words that are emphasized affect the meaning of those lines?

Lines and Stanzas in "View of a Lake"

You can also read William Carlos Williams's "View of a Lake" as though it were written in sentences. Finding the sentences in this poem may be more difficult than it was in "The Play" because the poem has no periods. It does have sentences, though. Some are complete sentences. Others are sentence fragments, or parts of sentences.

7. Look closely at the poem. How does Williams indicate the beginning of each sentence in "View of a Lake"? How many sentences (including sentence fragments) does the poem have?

The structure of "View of a Lake" differs from that of "The Play" in another way. "The Play" is not divided into stanzas. "View of a Lake" is broken into three-line stanzas.

Turn back to "The Cremation of Sam McGee." Compare its stanzas to those in "View of a Lake." Notice the differences in the length of the stanzas and in the line lengths.

8. What are the most obvious differences between the structure of "The Cremation of Sam McGee" and that of "View of a Lake"?

Now look closely at how the stanzas in the two poems end. In "The Cremation of Sam McGee" each stanza ends with the end of a sentence. You paused, almost as if taking a breath, before moving on to the next stanza.

In "View of a Lake" the stanzas produce the opposite effect. Each stanza ends in the middle of a sentence. Although the space signals a pause, the sentence pushes you forward across the space to the next stanza. There is a conflict between resting at the break and going on. You solve this conflict by holding on to the last word of the stanza, as if to carry it across the space. If you were to illustrate the effect, it might look like this:

> Where a
> waste of cinders
> slopes down tooooooo / the railroad and
> the lake
> stand three childrennnnnnn / beside the weed-grown
> chassis
> of a wrecked carrrrrrr / immobile in a line
> facing the water

9. What effect does that kind of reading have on the words at the beginning of each stanza? Are they read faster or slower?

By structuring "View of a Lake" in the way you have just seen, Williams produces an important effect. In each stanza he presents a distinct image, or picture, but as you move from one stanza to the next, the picture slowly changes. In the beginning of the poem you see a highway and a rock face. Then, as when a camera moves in for a close-up shot, you see new details in each stanza. As the features are added, the view evolves into a living scene. As each detail comes into view, a mood is created. <u>Mood</u> is the general feeling or atmosphere of the poem.

10. Choose three features that are added to the original view and explain what effect you think each has on the scene.

Reading "The Seven Ages of Man"

"The Seven Ages of Man" introduces you to another structure. Its lines are longer than those in the other two poems, and it contains punctuation such as commas, colons, semicolons, and periods. Like "The Play," however, the poem is not divided into stanzas.

Although "The Seven Ages of Man" uses language that is almost four hundred years old, it is quite easy to read once you know the meaning of a few old-fashioned words, which are explained in the Vocabulary section and in the footnotes. The poem is based on a <u>metaphor</u>—an imaginative implied comparison between two unlike things. The purpose of a metaphor is to give you an unusual way of looking at one of the things. A metaphor is a direct comparison that suggests one thing *is* another. Shakespeare makes the comparison in the first sentence. He speaks of the world as a stage and a man's life as the seven acts of a play. The rest of the poem lists and briefly describes each of those seven acts, or ages.

11. What are the seven ages that the poem identifies? According to the poem, what is a man like at each of those ages?

Meter. In "The Seven Ages of Man" the lines are not only longer than in the other two poems but they also have a definite meter. The basic meter is evident in these lines:

  ˘   ´   ˘   ´˘ ´ ˘   ´ ˘ ´
They have their exits and their entrances;
  ˘   ´   ˘   ´ ˘   ´   ˘   ´˘   ´
And one man in his time plays many parts.

As you learned in Chapter 1, each stressed syllable plus the un-stressed syllables that go with it make up a foot. There are different forms of metrical feet. Here you have one unstressed syllable followed by one stressed syllable. That kind of foot is called an <u>iamb</u>. In this poem there are five feet per line. A five-foot line is called <u>pentameter</u>. *Penta* comes from a Greek word meaning five. Five-foot lines in which each foot is an iamb are called <u>iambic pentameter</u>. In English poetry iambic pentameter is used more often than any other meter. All of Shakespeare's plays, for example, are written in iambic pentameter.

Variations in Rhythm. Although iambic pentameter is the basic rhythm of "The Seven Ages of Man," Shakespeare sometimes varies the pattern. A regular rhythm can become monotonous to the reader or listener. As you saw in Chapter 1, by breaking the regular rhythm, the poet draws attention to a word or syllable.

Look at the following line describing the schoolboy. Notice where the meter changes: "And shining morning face, creeping like snail." In that line the word *creeping* breaks the pattern, and you hear two stressed syllables followed by two unstressed ones: FACE CREEPing like. The change emphasizes the word *creeping* and focuses your attention on the schoolboy's reluctance to go to school.

12. In "The Seven Ages of Man" find at least two other lines in which Shakespeare varies the meter. In each case, what word and idea get added emphasis?

Another way that Shakespeare varies the rhythm is by adding an extra unstressed syllable from time to time:
  ˘   ´ ˘ ˘   ´ ˘   ´˘ ˘   ´ ˘   ´ ˘
His acts being seven ages. At first the infant

In two places the iambic foot is dropped in favor of the foot with two unstressed syllables. Another unusual feature is the extra unstressed syllable at the end of the line. Instead of ending on a stressed syllable, the line ends more gently on an unstressed note.

13. Find at least two other lines with extra unstressed syllables. Write each line, marking the stressed and unstressed syllables. In your own words describe the effect of those variations.

Blank Verse and Free Verse

If you reread all three poems, you will notice that not one has rhymed lines. Only in Shakespeare's poem do you find a definite meter—iambic pentameter. Unrhymed poetry that is written in iambic pentameter is known as blank verse. Many of the greatest works in English poetry are written in blank verse. Shakespeare and other great poets found that the unrhymed iambic lines of blank verse lend themselves well to serious subjects.

The other two poems, "The Play" and "View of a Lake," are examples of another form of poetry known as free verse. A poem written in free verse does not have any fixed meter, rhyme, or line length. The rhythm may vary from line to line or within a line. Occasionally, lines may rhyme. It is "free" because the poet is free to change the patterns or to use no pattern at all. Many twentieth-century poets have chosen to write in free verse.

Questions for Thought and Discussion

The questions and activities that follow will help you to explore the three poems in this chapter in more depth and at the same time develop your critical thinking skills.

1. **Examining Levels of Meaning.** Earlier in this chapter, you were asked what "The Play" might be about besides football. Divide the class into small groups. Each group should suggest several ideas about what other meanings the poem might have and then share them with the rest of the class.

2. **Analyzing Details.** Working alone or in small groups, make a summary of the scene described in "View of a Lake." Think about each detail in the poem before writing the summary.

3. **Identifying the Mood.** Mood is the feeling or atmosphere that the poet creates. "View of a Lake" is like a photograph. Its description is sharp and clear. As in a photograph, nothing moves. It is as if time stood still. The poem describes a rather ordinary scene, yet somehow there is a sense of mystery. What do you think is the mystery? How does the poet communicate that sense of mystery?

4. **Applying a Metaphor.** Shakespeare's poem describes seven stages in a man's life. Would the same seven stages apply to a woman's life? Explain how each "age" would apply to a woman or how it might be different.

Writing About Literature

Several suggestions for writing projects are given below. You may be asked to complete one or more of these projects. If you have any questions about how to begin a writing assignment, review Using the Writing Process, beginning on page 249.

1. **Writing About Rhythm.** Copy at least seven consecutive lines from "The Play." Mark each syllable as either stressed [/] or unstressed [∪]. Then write a paragraph explaining how the arrangement of stressed and unstressed syllables draws your attention to specific words and ideas.

2. **Describing a Scene in a Poem.** Look out your bedroom window or another window in your home. List six to ten things that you see and arrange the list in an order that makes sense to you. Then write a description of the scene in lines of poetry. To write the poem in such a way that the most important words stand out. Look at "View of a Lake" as a model.

3. **Writing a Summary.** Summarize the "seven ages" that Shakespeare includes in his poem. Then discuss whether you think a man today experiences similar stages or different ones.

Chapter 3

Selection

The Raven
EDGAR ALLAN POE

Lesson

Sound in Poetry

❖

About the Selection

A raven is a large black bird belonging to the crow family. It is a character in many ancient stories, and it is usually considered a symbol of bad luck. A symbol, you will recall, is a person, a place, or an object that stands for something other or more important than itself. In traditional folklore the raven was symbolic of bad luck, evil, and death.

This sinister bird is the central character in Edgar Allan Poe's poem "The Raven." The poem was first published in 1845 in the New York *Evening Mirror*. "The Raven" was successful almost immediately and was soon widely reprinted. Since then, it has never lost its appeal. Today it is not only Poe's best-known poem but also one of the best-known poems in American literature.

Why is "The Raven" still so popular? Perhaps you can answer that question after you have read the poem. Think about the atmosphere of mystery and foreboding that Poe creates. What effect does it have on you?

The poem begins with the narrator half-asleep, hearing—or thinking he hears—someone tapping at his door. Maybe you know how it feels to wake up knowing that some sound has disturbed your sleep but not knowing quite what it was. In "The Raven" the story becomes ominous as the sound continues. You soon realize that the narrator is in an unhappy, tortured state of mind.

Haunted, gloomy, and tormented poems and stories are a trademark of Edgar Allan Poe. He was born in Boston in 1809. His parents were actors who traveled a great deal. At the age of three, after his father deserted the family and his mother died, Poe became an orphan. He was raised by John and Frances Allan, a well-to-do couple whose name Poe later added to his own.

In 1826 Poe entered the University of Virginia. Although he did well in his studies, he ran up more debts than John Allan was willing to pay, and after one semester Poe was forced to leave. He then joined the army and eventually received an appointment to West Point. At West Point, however, Poe changed his mind about a military career. He stopped going to classes and was finally expelled. He was then twenty-two years old.

For the remaining eighteen years of his life, Poe worked as an editor and critic. He wrote articles, stories, and poems for various magazines. He had some success as a writer and editor but had never earned very much. Consequently, Poe and his wife lived in near poverty.

Poe's life was complicated by worries about his wife, Virginia, whom he married in 1836. She was an invalid who suffered from tuberculosis. After she died in 1847, Poe became very depressed, and his last years were grim. Many critics blamed his problems on his heavy drinking.

In 1849 Poe became engaged to a woman he had known since childhood. A short time before the wedding date, however, he was found lying on a street in Baltimore in a coma. He died without regaining consciousness. Poe was only forty years old.

Although Poe wrote both stories and poetry, he is probably best known today as the author of horror stories such as "The Tell-Tale Heart," "The Pit and the Pendulum," and "The Fall of the House of Usher." He is also credited with the early development of two other types of stories—the detective story and science fiction. Today an award called the "Edgar," in Poe's honor, is given each year to the author of the best mystery story.

Lesson Preview

The lesson that follows "The Raven" focuses on the effects of sound that Poe uses. Poets have different ways of using sound to give poetry a musical quality or to emphasize certain words and ideas. As you read this poem, listen closely to the sounds of the words. Read some stanzas aloud so that you actually hear their sound.

"The Raven" tells a gloomy, haunting story. The sounds of the poem contribute to the eerie feeling. The questions that follow will help you identify the ways in which Poe uses effects of sound. As you read, think about how you would answer these questions.

1 In each stanza, which words rhyme? Which words begin with the same sound?

2 What is the speaker's feeling at the beginning of the poem? In the middle of the poem? At the end of the poem?

3 What is the mood, or general atmosphere, of the poem?

4 How do the sounds of the words in the poem help to suggest different moods?

5 What happens in the poem? Pay particular attention to the stanzas where the speaker is talking to the Raven. Why is he asking the Raven certain questions? What does the Raven reply?

Vocabulary

Here are some difficult words that appear in the poem that follows. Study the words and their definitions, as well as the sentences that show how the words are used. This will help you get the most from your reading.

lore knowledge; learning. *By listening to the lore of the local townspeople, the researcher learned a great deal about the history of the region.*

surcease an end or cessation. *The prolific writer has had books on the best-seller list for ten years without surcease.*

obeisance a gesture of respect such as a bow. *The foreign visitor made his polite obeisance to the emperor.*

mien manner; appearance. *Although her face appeared serious, something in her mien convinced us that she was actually stifling a laugh.*

beguiling tricking; luring. *The salesman's beguiling smile and coaxing words almost tricked me into buying the car.*

decorum proper and dignified behavior. *The noisy and unruly pupils were punished for their lack of decorum.*

countenance the expression of the face. *Tears had replaced the smile that was usually present on Sue's countenance.*

discourse talk; conversation. *We were pleasantly surprised by the speaker's intelligent discourse on the country's economy.*

placid calm; quiet. *The blue sky and placid sea gave no hint of the approaching storm.*

dirges sad, slow pieces of music that show grief for the dead, as at a funeral. *Bill's poor piano playing made all his selections sound like depressing dirges.*

seraphim angels of the highest rank. *She decorated the card with drawings of seraphim and delicate vines.*

respite a period of temporary relief; pause. *Bob sought a respite from his own terrible cooking by making reservations at one of the best restaurants in the city.*

pallid pale; without much color. *Mary's pallid complexion soon improved after spending a few weeks in the fresh air of Vermont.*

The Raven

EDGAR ALLAN POE

Once upon a midnight dreary, while I pondered, weak and weary,
Over many a quaint and curious volume of forgotten lore—
While I nodded, nearly napping, suddenly there came a tapping,
As of someone gently rapping, rapping at my chamber door.
5   " 'Tis some visitor," I muttered, "tapping at my chamber door—
        Only this and nothing more."

Ah, distinctly I remember it was in the bleak December;
And each separate dying ember wrought its ghost upon the floor.
Eagerly I wished the morrow;— vainly I had sought to borrow
10 From my books surcease of sorrow—sorrow for the lost Lenore—
For the rare and radiant maiden whom the angels name Lenore—
        Nameless *here* for evermore.

And the silken, sad, uncertain rustling of each purple curtain
Thrilled me—filled me with fantastic terrors never felt before;
15 So that now, to still the beating of my heart, I stood repeating
" 'Tis some visitor entreating entrance at my chamber door—
Some late visitor entreating entrance at my chamber door;—
        This it is and nothing more."

Presently my soul grew stronger; hesitating then no longer,
20 "Sir," said I, "or Madam, truly your forgiveness I implore;
But the fact is I was napping, and so gently you came rapping,
And so faintly you came tapping, tapping at my chamber door,
That I scarce was sure I heard you"—here I opened wide the door;——
        Darkness there and nothing more.

25 Deep into that darkness peering, long I stood there wondering, fearing,
Doubting, dreaming dreams no mortal ever dared to dream before;
But the silence was unbroken, and the stillness gave no token,
And the only word there spoken was the whispered word, "Lenore?"
This I whispered, and an echo murmured back the word, "Lenore!"
30   Merely this and nothing more.

Back into the chamber turning, all my soul within me burning,
Soon again I heard a tapping somewhat louder than before.
"Surely," said I, "surely that is something at my window lattice;
Let me see, then, what thereat is, and this mystery explore—
35 Let my heart be still a moment and this mystery explore;—
        'Tis the wind and nothing more!"

Open here I flung the shutter, when, with many a flirt and flutter,
In there stepped a stately Raven of the saintly days of yore;
Not the least obeisance made he; not a minute stopped or stayed he;
40 But with mien of lord or lady, perched above my chamber door—
Perched upon a bust of Pallas[1] just above my chamber door—
        Perched, and sat, and nothing more.

Then this ebony bird beguiling my sad fancy into smiling,
By the grave and stern decorum of the countenance it wore,
45 "Though thy crest be shorn and shaven, thou," I said, "art sure no craven,[2]
Ghastly grim and ancient Raven wandering from the Nightly shore—
Tell me what thy lordly name is on the Night's Plutonian[3] shore!"
        Quoth the Raven "Nevermore."

---

1. **Pallas:** a reference to Pallas Athena or simply Athena, the Greek goddess of wisdom and the arts.
2. **craven:** coward.   3. **Plutonian:** having to do with Pluto, the Roman god of the dead and ruler of the underworld.

Much I marveled this ungainly fowl to hear discourse so plainly,
50 Though its answer little meaning—little relevancy bore;
For we cannot help agreeing that no living human being
Ever yet was blessed with seeing bird above his chamber door—
Bird or beast upon the sculptured bust above his chamber door,
        With such name as "Nevermore."

55 But the Raven, sitting lonely on the placid bust, spoke only
That one word, as if his soul in that one word he did outpour.
Nothing farther then he uttered—not a feather then he fluttered—
Till I scarcely more than muttered, "Other friends have flown before—
On the morrow *he* will leave me, as my Hopes have flown before."
60   Then the bird said "Nevermore."

Startled at the stillness broken by reply so aptly spoken,
"Doubtless," said I, "what it utters is its only stock and store
Caught from some unhappy master whom unmerciful Disaster
Followed fast and followed faster till his songs one burden bore—
65 Till the dirges of his Hope that melancholy burden bore
        Of 'Never—nevermore.' "

But the Raven still beguiling my sad fancy into smiling,
Straight I wheeled a cushioned seat in front of bird, and bust and door;
Then, upon the velvet sinking, I betook myself to linking
70 Fancy unto fancy, thinking what this ominous bird of yore—
What this grim, ungainly, ghastly, gaunt and ominous bird of yore
        Meant in croaking "Nevermore."

Sound in Poetry

This I sat engaged in guessing, but no syllable expressing
To the fowl whose fiery eyes now burned into my bosom's core;
75 This and more I sat divining, with my head at ease reclining
On the cushion's velvet lining that the lamp-light gloated o'er,
But whose velvet-violet lining with the lamp-light gloating o'er,
          She shall press, ah, nevermore!

Then, methought, the air grew denser, perfumed from an unseen censer[4]
80 Swung by seraphim whose foot-falls tinkled on the tufted floor.
"Wretch!" I cried, "thy God hath lent thee—by these angels he hath sent thee
Respite—respite and nepenthe[5] from the memories of Lenore;
Quaff, oh quaff this kind nepenthe and forget this lost Lenore!"
          Quoth the Raven "Nevermore."

85 "Prophet!" said I, "thing of evil!—prophet still, if bird or devil!
Whether Tempter sent, or whether tempest tossed thee here ashore,
Desolate yet all undaunted, on this desert land enchanted—
On this home by Horror haunted—tell me truly, I implore—
Is there—*is* there balm in Gilead?[6]—tell me—tell me, I implore!"
90   Quoth the Raven "Nevermore."

"Prophet!" said I, "thing of evil!—prophet still, if bird or devil!
By that Heaven that bends above us—by that God we both adore—
Tell this soul with sorrow laden if, within the distant Aidenn,[7]
It shall clasp a sainted maiden whom the angels name Lenore—
95 Clasp a rare and radiant maiden whom the angels name Lenore."
          Quoth the Raven "Nevermore."

4. censer: a container in which incense is burned. **5. nepenthe:** a potion used to induce forgetfulness of pain and grief. **6. balm in Gilead:** these words come from the Biblical lines, "Is there no balm in Gilead, no physician there?" (Jeremiah 8:22) A balm is a healing ointment; Gilead is a region in what is now Jordan, east of Israel. Here the expression means, Is there any relief? **7. Aidenn:** the Garden of Eden. Here, the word is used in the sense of heaven, or paradise.

"Be that word our sign of parting, bird or fiend!" I shrieked, upstarting—
"Get thee back into the tempest and the Night's Plutonian shore!
Leave no black plume as a token of that lie thy soul hath spoken!
100 Leave my loneliness unbroken!—quit the bust above my door!
Take thy beak from out my heart, and take thy form from off my door!"
              Quoth the Raven "Nevermore."

And the Raven, never flitting, still is sitting, *still* is sitting
On the pallid bust of Pallas just above my chamber door;
105 And his eyes have all the seeming of a demon's that is dreaming,
And the lamp-light o'er him streaming throws his shadow on the floor;
And my soul from out that shadow that lies floating on the floor
              Shall be lifted—nevermore!

Reviewing the Selection

Answer each of the following questions. You may look back at the poem if necessary.

Recalling Facts

1. The Raven enters the room through
   - ☐ a. a door.
   - ☐ b. a window.
   - ☐ c. the chimney.
   - ☐ d. a trapdoor.

Understanding Main Ideas

2. The Raven says that the speaker will never
   - ☐ a. get over the death of Lenore.
   - ☐ b. meet another girl like Lenore.
   - ☐ c. be able to understand life.
   - ☐ d. finish reading his quaint and curious volumes of forgotten lore.

Placing Events in Order

3. The speaker opens the door of his chamber
   - ☐ a. before the Raven comes in the window.
   - ☐ b. after the Raven comes in the window.
   - ☐ c. just before the Raven leaves.
   - ☐ d. just after the Raven says "Nevermore" for the first time.

Finding Supporting Details

4. After the speaker opens the door and finds no one there, who does he think might have been there?
   - ☐ a. a friend
   - ☐ b. Lenore
   - ☐ c. the Raven
   - ☐ d. Edgar Allan Poe

5. "Quaff, oh quaff this kind nepenthe and forget this lost Lenore!" In this context *quaff* means
   ☐ a. quote.
   ☐ b. throw away.
   ☐ c. enjoy.
   ☐ d. drink.

Interpreting the Selection

Answer each of the following questions. You may look back at the poem if necessary.

6. From what the speaker says about Lenore, you can infer that she
   ☐ a. has run away.
   ☐ b. is dead.
   ☐ c. is his sister.
   ☐ d. has been murdered.

7. The line "Then this ebony bird beguiling my sad fancy into smiling" indicates that the speaker's first reaction to the Raven is
   ☐ a. amusement.
   ☐ b. puzzlement.
   ☐ c. fear.
   ☐ d. awe.

8. In the first two stanzas the author's purpose is to
   - ☐ a. amuse the reader.
   - ☐ b. frighten the reader.
   - ☐ c. talk about the Raven's appearance.
   - ☐ d. establish a mood of gloom and foreboding.

9. How is the speaker's mood in the last stanza different from his mood at the beginning of the poem? He is
   - ☐ a. happier.
   - ☐ b. angrier.
   - ☐ c. more despairing.
   - ☐ d. hopeful.

10. The Raven's refusal to leave is a sign that the
    - ☐ a. speaker is going crazy.
    - ☐ b. bird is more comfortable perched on Pallas than in his last home.
    - ☐ c. speaker will never get over his loss of Lenore.
    - ☐ d. bird is tired of being out in the cold December weather.

Sound in Poetry

In the first two chapters you looked at the effects of meter and the arrangement of lines in poetry. In this lesson you will see how Edgar Allan Poe uses the sounds of words to create effects in "The Raven." In poetry the sound of individual words and the repetition of sounds are very important. Poets choose each word carefully. Often they use a particular word or phrase for the way it sounds.

A word's sound can create a particular effect. A word can be harsh, gentle, or even merry. Depending on its sound, a word or phrase can influence the mood, or feeling, of a poem. The repetition of a sound can emphasize a thought or an image. Sounds can also build <u>suspense</u>—the interest, excitement, and anticipation that you feel about what will happen in the poem.

Reading "The Raven"

Before examining the sounds of the poem, you need to understand the poem's general mood. Like "The Cremation of Sam McGee," "The Raven" is a narrative poem. And it, too, tells an odd story. The two poems are also alike in that the speaker is involved in the story.

In the first line of "The Raven," you learn that the story takes place "upon a midnight dreary," and that the speaker's state of mind is "weak and weary." Both phrases help to fix the mood by establishing a gloomy setting and a dejected speaker.

Two lines later, a mysterious tapping begins, and the story of "The Raven" is under way. The speaker tells himself that it is only a "visitor." When he adds, "Only this and nothing more," you feel the suspense. Somehow you know that the tapping will turn out to be something other than a visit from a friend.

In the second and third stanzas, you learn more about the time and the place of the story and about the speaker's mental state.

1. What additional details about the setting are given in stanzas 2 and 3?

In the fourth stanza the speaker gathers his courage and opens the door. He finds only "Darkness there and nothing more." The fifth stanza tells how that makes him feel and what he does.

2. In your own words summarize how the speaker feels in the fifth stanza.

When the speaker again hears tapping, he opens the window, and in steps the Raven. It goes straight to a perch on the bust of Pallas above the door. The speaker is disturbed by that development, but he tries to make light of it. He asks the bird its name. The speaker speaks to the bird five more times in the course of the poem. The bird gives the same response to each of the speaker's statements.

3. In your own words state what the speaker says each of the five times. What do the speaker's words tell you about his state of mind?

In the last stanza the story shifts from that "midnight dreary" of a long-ago "bleak December" to the time when the poem is being written. You learn that the bird is still there and that the speaker will never escape its spell.

4. What do you think the last stanza means?

Rhyme

Poe reinforces the mood and suspense in the narrative with various kinds of effects of sound. The most common effect of sound is the use of words that rhyme. Rhyme is the repetition of the same or similar stressed sound or sounds. It is often related to the meaning of a poem because it brings two or more words together.

Rhyme is used so often in poetry that some people think all poetry must rhyme, or that anything that rhymes is poetry. Both beliefs are false. As you saw in Chapter 2, poetry does not have to rhyme. In addition, putting together a few words that rhyme does not necessarily make a poem.

Rhyme is a common feature of poetry and has various forms. In "The Raven," Poe uses rhyme in several different ways.

End Rhyme. In most poems that rhyme the repetition of syllable sounds occurs at the ends of lines. That is called <u>end rhyme</u>. In "The Raven" you will find a typical pattern of end rhyme.

One of the most important words in "The Raven" is *nevermore*. In eleven of the poem's stanzas, *nevermore* is the last word. Of the remaining seven stanzas, one ends in the word *evermore* and six with the phrase *nothing more*. Within each stanza, you will find several lines that end with words that rhyme with *more*. End rhyme gives the poem a musical, or rhythmic, pattern.

5. *Look at the first stanza. What word ends the stanza? What lines in that stanza rhyme? What words end those lines?*

In the first stanza four of the lines end in the same sound. That rhyming pattern is repeated throughout the poem.

Rhyme Scheme. The poem has a <u>rhyme scheme</u> if the words at the ends of two or more lines rhyme. Rhyme scheme adds to the musical sound of poetry and affects the mood of the poem. The usual way of indicating a rhyme scheme of a poem is to assign a different letter of the alphabet to the final sound of each line within a stanza. Read the stanza below. Notice that each line is given a letter of the alphabet. If the last word in a line rhymes with another line, they are given the same letter.

Once upon a midnight dreary, while I pondered weak and weary,	*a*
Over many a quaint and curious volume of forgotten lore—	*b*
While I nodded, nearly napping, suddenly there came a tapping,	*c*
As of someone gently rapping, rapping at my chamber door.	*b*
" 'Tis some visitor," I muttered, "tapping at my chamber door—	*b*
Only this and nothing more."	*b*

The rhyme scheme for the first stanza of "The Raven" is *abcbbb*. The first line is given the letter *a*. Since no other lines end with a word that rhymes with *weary*, that is the only *a* line. Line 2 and all lines that rhyme with it are given the letter *b*. The third line, ending with the word *tapping*, is given the letter *c*.

6. List the words that end the second, fourth, fifth, and sixth lines of at least two stanzas in "The Raven." How would you describe the way they sound—cheerful? solemn? bright? Find a word or two to describe the sound.

Internal Rhyme. Although rhymes are usually found at the ends of lines, they can also occur within a line. Repetition of end sounds *within* a line is called <u>internal rhyme</u>. For example, look at the first line of stanza 1. The repetition of sound within the line helps to emphasize both ideas— *dreary* and *weary.* Look at the first lines of every stanza. Notice how Poe uses internal rhyme to stress certain words and to increase the rhythmic pattern of the poem.

Feminine and Masculine Rhymes. Two types of rhyme that add to the rhythm and meaning of a poem are feminine and masculine rhyme. Rhymes that consist of a stressed syllable followed by one or two un-stressed syllables *(breaking, taking)* are called <u>feminine rhymes</u>. Rhymes of one stressed syllable *(lore, door, more)* are called <u>masculine rhymes</u>.

Read the following stanza. Notice that the first and third lines contain feminine rhyme; that is, they end with words of two or three syllables with the first syllable stressed and they rhyme with words within that line. The last three lines end with masculine rhymes—one stressed syllable—and they rhyme with each other. Masculine and feminine rhyme can occur as internal or end rhymes.

> Presently my soul grew STRONGer; hesitating then no LONGer,
> "Sir," said I, "or Madam, truly your forgiveness I implore;
> But the fact is I was NAPPing, and so gently you came RAPPing,
> And so faintly you came tapping, tapping at my chamber DOOR,
> That I scarce was sure I heard you"—here I opened wide the DOOR;—
> Darkness there and nothing MORE.

Feminine rhyme can also consist of two or more words that rhyme. Lines 39 and 40 of stanza 7, for example, contain the rhymes *made he, stayed he,* and *lady.*

Feminine rhyme adds a lightness and grace to poetry, especially when it is used with the sharp, strong sounds of masculine rhyme. Poe uses the contrast between feminine and masculine rhyme not only to enrich the mood but also to contribute to the meaning of the words in the poem.

7. List two other examples of feminine rhyme in "The Raven."

Repetition and Rhyme

In "The Raven" Poe creates strong sound effects by using repetition.

Look at the first stanza again. Notice that lines 4 and 5 end with the word *door.* Repeating *door* does not really make a rhyme. To be a rhyme, the repeated syllables should have different beginning sounds, such as *lore* and *door.*

However, if you look at the middle of lines 4 and 5, you find a rhyme with the words *rapping* and *tapping.* Each of those rhyming words is followed by the same phrase: *at my chamber door.* The effect of the rhyme and of the repetition is to link the two lines closely.

8. Choose another stanza in which repetition occurs. What words are repeated? What is the effect of the repetition?

Alliteration. A sound effect related to rhyme is alliteration. Alliteration is a device of repetition and makes a sound pattern by repeating the same first sounds in words, usually consonant sounds.

Alliteration appears throughout "The Raven." In line 1 you hear that the narrator is weak and weary. In line 2 the old books are quaint and curious. (As this example shows, it is the first *sound,* and not the first letter, that matters.) In line 3 you have a three-word alliteration: "While I nodded nearly napping . . ."

Alliteration can have a pleasant and musical sound, or it can sound harsh and jangling. Poets use alliteration to add emphasis to an idea or to certain words, or to heighten the mood of a line or a stanza.

Sometimes Poe seems to build an entire line from two or three sounds, as in this line from stanza 5: "Doubting, dreaming dreams no mortal ever dared to dream before."

9. Say the line aloud a few times. Let it roll on your tongue. What three consonant sounds does Poe repeat? What effect does the sound of the line have?

10. "The Raven" has many examples of alliteration. Find three examples whose sounds you particularly like. Explain why you chose each and how each contributes to the mood of the poem.

Consonance. A different sound effect that is similar to alliteration but more subtle is consonance. Consonance occurs in words where the consonant-sounds stay the same but the vowel-sounds are different *(pitter, patter* and *spin, spun).* Notice the use of consonance in line 45: " '*Though thy* crest be *shorn* and *shaven . . .*' "

Assonance. Another subtle device used for sound effect is assonance— the repetition of similar vowel sounds within words. Look at this line from stanza 2: "For the rare and radiant maiden whom the angels name Lenore." Like alliteration and other kinds of repetition, assonance is used to emphasize certain sounds and to give a musical quality to the lines.

Poe uses assonance and consonance less often than alliteration. However, they do appear in several stanzas.

Read the stanza below and answer the question that follows.

Open here I flung the shutter, when, with many a flirt and flutter,
In there stepped a stately Raven of the saintly days of yore;
Not the least obeisance made he; not a minute stopped or stayed he;
But with mien of lord or lady, perched above my chamber door—
Perched upon a bust of Pallas just above my chamber door—
   Perched, and sat, and nothing more.

11. Using the above stanza, identify examples of alliteration, consonance, and assonance. Identify the rhyme scheme. List examples of feminine and masculine rhyme.

Onomatopoeia

Many English words imitate the sounds or actions they name. *Splash, thud, honk, boom, hiss, peep,* and *buzz* are examples. The use of words whose sounds imitate, echo, or suggest their meanings is called onomatopoeia (on-uh-maht-uh-PEE-uh). Notice the sound of the word *tinkled* in this line from stanza 14: "Swung by seraphim whose foot-falls tinkled on the tufted floor."

Poets and other writers have several reasons for choosing words whose sounds suggest their meanings. Sometimes they use onomatopoeia to add humor. "Hickory dickory dock," in the nursery rhyme, humorously suggests the tick-tock of a clock. Poets also use onomatopoeia to reinforce the meaning of a line, or to create a picture in your mind.

12. Read the following line from stanza 3 aloud: "And the silken, sad, uncertain rustling of each purple curtain." What onomatopoeic word do you find in that line?

13. Find another example of onomatopoeia in "The Raven." What sound does it imitate or suggest?

Questions for Thought and Discussion

The questions and activities that follow will help you explore "The Raven" in more depth and at the same time develop your critical thinking skills.

1. **Supporting an Opinion.** How do the sound effects in "The Raven'" influence the mood of the poem?

2. **Comparing.** Compare the speakers, settings, and moods of "The Raven" and "The Cremation of Sam McGee." How are they similar? How are they different?

3. **Analyzing Character.** A magazine once published a cartoon showing Edgar Allan Poe writing "The Raven." Poe was staring off into space, chewing his pencil, and imagining various animals—a pig, a dog, a horse, a squirrel, a bat. Each was saying "Nevermore." What creature,

other than a raven, do you think might have worked in this poem? Think of two or three possibilities. What advantages and disadvantages might each have had compared to a raven?

4. **Inferring.** Pallas, or Athena, is the Greek goddess of wisdom and the arts. Why do you think Poe has the Raven perch on a bust of Pallas instead of on a bust of George Washington or another figure?

5. **Interpreting.** Look at the last stanza of "The Raven." How can a soul be trapped by a shadow? What does the speaker mean here?

Writing About Literature

Several suggestions for writing projects are given below. You may be asked to complete one or more of these projects. If you have any questions about how to begin a writing assignment, review Using the Writing Process, beginning on page 249.

1. **Summarizing.** Summarize how the speaker's state of mind changes in the course of his conversation with the Raven. What stages does he go through?

2. **Explaining.** "The Raven" is one of the best-known poems in English. What accounts for its popularity? Describe two or three characteristics of "The Raven" that might explain why the poem is still popular almost 150 years after it was written.

3. **Creating a Dialogue.** Suppose that the speaker in "The Raven" decided to take his problem to a friend or counselor. Imagine what they might say to each other and then write a part of their conversation. How would the speaker describe his situation? What kind of questions would the friend or counselor ask, and what advice would that person give?

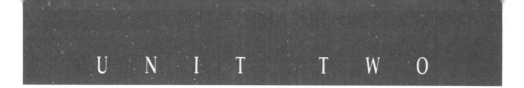

Seeing Poetry

*P*oetry is meant to be read slowly and carefully. Usually, it is intended to be heard as well as read. You cannot skim a poem to find its main ideas. Because poetry is so compact, every word is essential.

Most poems are made up of a series of images. An image is a representation of a person or thing, or a mental picture of something. A photograph is one kind of image. A photograph of your grandmother, for example, is a representation of her. Looking at the photograph is not the same as seeing her in person, but the representation does help to create a mental picture of her. Then your mind goes to work, filling in ideas, feelings, and thoughts about her that are not in the picture. The picture may bring to mind the sound of your grandmother's voice, her way of moving about a room, her likes and dislikes, and, more important, your feelings about her.

Images in poetry work in a similar way. In poetry an <u>image</u> is a word or phrase that creates a mental picture of something in your mind. To get the most from reading a poem, you do not simply look at the words and then read on. Instead, you let the word picture that the poet has created enter your mind. While you picture the image, you should ask yourself certain questions. Why is a specific picture—or image—created in your mind? What sights, sounds, and feelings does the poet add to that picture? Using only a few words, a poet can create an instant picture, complete with sight, sound, taste, smell, and touch.

In Unit Two you will look at the various ways in which poets create vivid and powerful images. As you will see, poets create all kinds of images, and each poet uses images in different ways to achieve different effects.

Chapter 4

❖

About the Selections

On a hillside overlooking the Rock River in northwestern Illinois is a fifty-foot statue of an American Indian named Black Hawk. He stands with his arms folded across his chest and gazes over the river valley into the distance.

Black Hawk was the chief of the Sauk and Fox tribes that once lived in the Rock River area in Illinois. In 1832 he and his people, in an attempt to preserve their land and their way of life, fought white settlers and soldiers moving into Illinois. The Indians fought bravely but they were outnumbered by the settlers. Black Hawk and the surviving Indians were driven westward to a reservation across the Mississippi River.

In the first poem "Illinois: At Night, Black Hawk's Statue Broods," the statue of Black Hawk speaks. In the poem you read Black Hawk's thoughts as he stands, immobile, gazing across the landscape.

J. W. Rivers, who wrote this poem, is noted for his sympathetic treatment of subjects related to American Indians. He was born in 1934 in Chicago, Illinois, but he lived in Mexico for many years. During that time, his interest in and concern for Indians—the Indians of Mexico, Central America, Brazil, and the United States—grew. His concern is reflected in much of his poetry. Rivers writes poetry in both English and Spanish. He also writes short stories, mostly in Spanish.

The second poem in this chapter is "Not Seeing Is Believing." Like "Black Hawk," it was also written in the twentieth century. Its author, Paul Petrie, was born in Detroit in 1928. Since 1959, he has taught English at the University of Rhode Island. Over the years, Petrie has published a large number of poems as well as several collections of poems. He describes his poetry as "lyrical [songlike], relatively emotional, dramatic." He adds that he thinks of a poem as an "act of praise." As you read "Not Seeing Is Believing," think about the ways in which Petrie uses language to show the beauty of a simple event.

The last two poems in this lesson are by well-known English poets. William Wordsworth (1770–1850), who wrote "Daffodils," was an English romantic poet. When he began writing in the 1790s, most poetry was written in a formal, stiff, and artificial language. Many people thought that only subjects that dealt with the mind, order, and logic were appropriate for serious poetry.

In 1798 Wordsworth and a friend, poet Samuel Taylor Coleridge, challenged the traditional attitude toward poetry by publishing a book of poems called *Lyrical Ballads*. In the introduction to the book, they stated that serious poetry could—and should—be written about ordinary subjects and in everyday language. They believed that poetry is created by emotions that come from actual experience.

Both Wordsworth and Coleridge were well-known poets, and their ideas were adopted by others. Today the publication of *Lyrical Ballads* is considered a major turning point in the history of English poetry.

Wordsworth loved the outdoors. He took long walks and often wrote about the scenes of natural beauty he saw. "Daffodils" tells of an experience with nature and its effect on him.

Among the poets influenced by Wordsworth's ideas was John Keats. He was born in 1795, twenty-five years after Wordsworth. Keats began writing poetry when he was fifteen years old. At twenty-two he published his first collection of poems. The poems were not well received, but Keats continued to write. Some of his best poems were written during the following year. In 1819 Keats became seriously ill with tuberculosis, and he died in 1821 at the age of twenty-five.

Despite his brief career, Keats is considered by many scholars to be one of the finest poets of the romantic period. After you read "On the Grasshopper and Cricket," see if you can find similarities between Wordsworth's and Keats's views of the natural world.

Lesson Preview

The lesson that follows the four poems focuses on the various ways that poets create images, or pictures, in your mind. As you read each poem, stop whenever the poet describes something that you can picture in your mind. Think for a moment about the picture in your mind and how it relates to the poem.

The questions that follow will help you find the images in the four poems. As you read, think about how you would answer these questions.

1 In "Illinois: At Night, Black Hawk's Statue Broods," the poet mentions a number of specific items. What picture does each item bring to your mind?

2 In "Not Seeing Is Believing" notice how the characters introduced at the beginning are developed. How does your view of those characters change in the course of the poem?

3 In "Daffodils" the poet describes a scene he once saw on a walk in the country. What effect did that experience have on him? Why did it have such a lasting effect?

4 In the last poem, "On the Grasshopper and Cricket," the poet appeals to at least three of the five senses. To which senses does he appeal?

Images and Imagery

Vocabulary

Here are some difficult words that appear in the poems that follow. Study the words and their definitions, as well as the sentences that show how the words are used. This will help you get the most from your reading.

buzzard a kind of hawk. *The hungry buzzard circled over a flock of chickens.*

pondering thinking deeply about something. *Because the project contained so many errors, Sue spent a lot of time pondering over the best ways to fix them.*

sprightly lively; full of energy. *The sprightly little mountain goat leaped quickly and easily over the rocky crevices.*

bliss great joy or happiness. *After George ate his third piece of pie, he leaned back in his chair and sighed in contented bliss.*

Illinois: At Night,
Black Hawk's Statue Broods

J. W. RIVERS
For Robt. D. Sutherland

The forests I believed in,
Where pathways were open,
Come to this:
Duck decoys,
5   Picnic tables,
Oak furniture,
Faces in mirrors.

Where is my father,
Who thrived
10   On a trickle of water,
Could feast
On skunk or buzzard?

My mother, whose hands,
Weaving like sand in the wind,
15   Took in birds
To mend their broken wings?

The land is old and tired,
It sleeps in its own shadow.

I cannot kneel
20   To touch the soil.
The wind in my ears
Makes everywhere
And nowhere
My home.

Not Seeing Is Believing

PAUL PETRIE

From across the stream, on the side of the opposite hill,
I see a woman in a blue, wool coat who is walking her dog.
Her hair is as white as snow, and her dog snow-white.
They are walking through the plum-brown, silvery branches of trees.

5   Step after step she moves,
leaning on each foot as the old do.
She is walking her dog and thinking.

Under the nest of her hair is another world—
are many other worlds—present, past, future—
10   but none of this shows.

She is walking her dog and thinking, and the dog too
is thinking—Bushes are telling damp, excited tales
of an earlier sun, of a darkness before this sun—

and the trees around them are thinking—slow, wooden thoughts
15   that stretch over centuries, and the earth in which the trees
root down also is pondering—deep, stone thoughts—
but none of this shows.

I see a woman in a blue, wool coat
who is walking a small, white dog
20   through the plum-brown, silvery trees.

Daffodils

WILLIAM WORDSWORTH

I wandered lonely as a cloud
   That floats on high o'er vales and hills,
When all at once I saw a crowd,
   A host, of golden daffodils,
5 Beside the lake, beneath the trees,
Fluttering and dancing in the breeze.

Continuous as the stars that shine
   And twinkle on the milky way,
They stretched in never-ending line
10   Along the margin of a bay:
Ten thousand saw I at a glance
Tossing their heads in sprightly dance.

The waves beside them danced, but they
   Out-did the sparkling waves in glee:
15 A Poet could not but be gay
   In such a jocund[1] company!
I gazed—and gazed—but little thought
What wealth the show to me had brought:

For oft, when on my couch I lie
20   In vacant or in pensive mood,
They flash upon that inward eye
   Which is the bliss of solitude;
And then my heart with pleasure fills,
And dances with the daffodils.

---

1. **jocund:** merry.

On the Grasshopper and Cricket

JOHN KEATS

The poetry of earth is never dead:
When all the birds are faint with the hot sun,
And hide in cooling trees, a voice will run
From hedge to hedge about the new-mown mead;[1]
5   That is the Grasshopper's—he takes the lead
In summer luxury,—he has never done
With his delights; for when tired out with fun
He rests at ease beneath some pleasant weed.

The poetry of earth is ceasing never:
10   On a lone winter evening, when the frost
Has wrought a silence, from the stove there shrills
The Cricket's song, in warmth increasing ever,
And seems to one in drowsiness half lost,
The Grasshopper's among some grassy hills.

1. **mead:** meadow.

Reviewing the Selections

Answer each of the following questions. You may look back at the poems if necessary.

Recalling Facts

1. In "Not Seeing Is Believing" the woman is wearing
   ☐ a. a long fur coat.
   ☐ b. a yellow raincoat.
   ☐ c. blue sneakers.
   ☐ d. a blue wool coat.

Understanding Main Ideas

2. A main idea of "Illinois: At Night, Black Hawk's Statue Broods" is that
   ☐ a. the land where Black Hawk once lived has changed.
   ☐ b. people in Illinois have put up statues to the past.
   ☐ c. the forest looks different at night than during the day.
   ☐ d. the Indians loved the land, and people today do not.

Placing Events in Order

3. In "On the Grasshopper and Cricket" the grasshopper's voice is heard
   ☐ a. along with the cricket's.
   ☐ b. in summer.
   ☐ c. every morning.
   ☐ d. when it rains.

Finding Supporting Details

4. In "Daffodils" the line "Fluttering and dancing in the breeze" refers to
   ☐ a. vales and hills.
   ☐ b. daffodils.
   ☐ c. a lake.
   ☐ d. trees.

Images and Imagery

5. "For oft, when on my couch I lie / In vacant or in <u>pensive</u> mood." In this context *pensive* means
   ☐ a. worried.
   ☐ b. poetic.
   ☐ c. independent.
   ☐ d. thoughtful.

Interpreting the Selections

Answer each of the following questions. You may look back at the poems if necessary.

Making Inferences

6. From the first stanza of "Illinois: At Night, Black Hawk's Statue Broods," you can infer that the statue is located
   ☐ a. outside a school.
   ☐ b. in a cornfield.
   ☐ c. in or near a park.
   ☐ d. close to an airport.

Analyzing the Evidence

7. On the evidence of "On the Grasshopper and Cricket," crickets
   ☐ a. live indoors in winter.
   ☐ b. look like grasshoppers.
   ☐ c. hide in cooling trees.
   ☐ d. eat weeds.

8. In "Not Seeing Is Believing" one of the author's purposes is to suggest that
   - ☐ a. there is more to an individual than his or her appearance.
   - ☐ b. dogs are good company for elderly people.
   - ☐ c. walking among trees helps people to think.
   - ☐ d. taking walks is good exercise for both the old and the young.

9. At the end of both "Daffodils" and "On the Grasshopper and Cricket," the poets are
   - ☐ a. concerned that natural beauty is being destroyed.
   - ☐ b. wishing they could spend more time outdoors with nature.
   - ☐ c. happily thinking back to an earlier experience with nature.
   - ☐ d. sorry that the summer is over.

10. In "Daffodils" the speaker
   - ☐ a. has never seen daffodils before.
   - ☐ b. has never liked daffodils until now.
   - ☐ c. is cheered by the memory of the field of daffodils he once saw.
   - ☐ d. prefers daffodils to any other kind of flower.

Images and Imagery

All writers try to communicate an idea or thought to you. Writers of nonfiction, such as journalists and biographers, want to give you information on their interpretation of certain facts and events. Writers of fiction, such as novelists and short-story writers, want to tell you about an experience in a unique and powerful way. Poets, too, want to share their experiences or their views of the world.

To share those ideas, poets use images to re-create an experience, an impression, or a mood. As you read in the introduction to Unit Two, an image is a word or phrase that creates a picture in your mind. Although many images are visual, an image can appeal to any of the other senses as well—sound, smell, taste, and touch. Some images appeal to more than one sense at the same time.

Good poets are skillful at creating and developing images. Sometimes a poet will try to create a scene or a feeling wholly through images. All the poetic word pictures, or images, in a poem are called <u>imagery</u>.

In this lesson you will learn some of the ways in which poets use imagery. You will also compare the ways in which the four poets you have just read use imagery.

Images and Concrete Language

One way that poets re-create an impression or sensory experience is by using a specific image that people can identify easily. To call up an image in your mind, a poet uses <u>concrete language</u>—words that describe things that you know and understand with your senses. Concrete language describes something that actually exists and can be seen or touched in your mind. For example, *airplane, rose,* and *book* are concrete words. *Bravery, justice,* and *beauty* are abstract words. The qualities that abstract words express do not physically exist, and they do not create a vivid image in your mind.

J. W. Rivers uses concrete language to create specific images in "Illinois: At Night, Black Hawk's Statue Broods." In the first stanza, for example, Black Hawk's brooding spirit says that the forests he once knew have become something else. He lists four items:

> Duck decoys,   Oak furniture,
> Picnic tables,   Faces in mirrors.

Each of those items is described in concrete language and each brings a specific picture to mind. Everyone who reads the names of those objects will get a similar mental picture, or image. For example, you will probably imagine a standard wooden picnic table with benches. Because that image identifies one particular thing, it is said to be specific. It is also concrete because it refers to a real object.

Taken together, the four images create a larger mental picture of what has become of the forest that Black Hawk once knew. The poet could have chosen to describe the land in great detail—the houses, cars, people, and so on. Such a description, however, would require many more words. Instead, in four short phrases, a total of nine words—Rivers creates an image in your mind of what Black Hawk's forest looks like today.

1. Describe a familiar scene in complete sentences. Then create an image of that same scene in poetic form. Use concrete language to develop a specific image of that scene.

Connotations

Poets must choose their words carefully because poetry uses so few words to create an image or express an idea. Each word has to be effective. Every word has a <u>denotation</u>, or dictionary meaning. Many words also have a connotation—the emotion that a word arouses or the meanings that it suggests in addition to its denotation, or dictionary meaning.

A word's connotation can come from the way it has been used over time. For example, the word *house* denotes a place where you live, but the word *home* connotes, or suggests, a warmer, cozier feeling; *coast* denotes the land next to water, but *seashore* suggests the salty smell of the air, the sights and sounds of the water, and the feel of the sand.

A word's connotation also comes from its context, or how the words that come before or after it influence its meaning. Compare the word *morning* in the next two sentences. "Each day has a *morning,* an afternoon, and an evening." "There will be another *morning,* another dawn." In the first sentence *morning* denotes a time of day. In the second sentence *morning* is influenced by the words around it and suggests a new beginning filled with freshness and energy. Often poets will use a particular word because its connotation reinforces the feeling that they are trying to create. A word can suggest certain emotions or ideas beyond its basic meaning and can create a strong image.

Think about the associations you make with the phrase "picnic tables." Perhaps you think of the four phrases, "duck decoys," "picnic tables," "oak furniture," and "faces in mirrors." When you put all four images together, you can actually see the contrast between the present-day forest and Black Hawk's forest.

2. Reread stanzas 2 and 3. What are the connotations of the words father, thrived, feast, mother, hands, *and* wind?

Contrasting Images

In the first stanza of "Illinois: At Night, Black Hawk's Statue Broods," the poet sets up a powerful picture of a changed land. It has been altered almost beyond recognition from what Black Hawk left behind in 1832.

Just how great is the change? In the next two stanzas, Rivers points out the contrast by creating more images. In them, he shows the relationship of the Indians to the land and the natural world. The Indians accepted what the land gave them. In return, they honored the land.

3. How do the specific images of Black Hawk's father and mother reveal the relationship between the Indians and the land?

4. In the fourth stanza Black Hawk describes the land as "old and tired," adding that it "sleeps in its own shadow." What does that image suggest to you?

5. Think about the image of the wind in the final stanza of the poem. Explain how it "makes everywhere and nowhere" Black Hawk's home.

Developing Images

In the poem "Not Seeing Is Believing," Paul Petrie also uses concrete language to develop specific images. As he develops the poem, he builds his images. In the first stanza, he introduces three elements in three separate images: a "woman in a blue, wool coat"; her "dog snow-white"; and "the plum-brown, silvery branches of trees."

In the next four stanzas the poet enlarges on those images. The second stanza, for example, describes how the old woman walks, and adds a new element: she is thinking. The word *thinking* leads to a new image in the next stanza: "Under the nest of her hair is another world."

6. What is that other world? Why isn't it obvious as part of the visual image?

The images of the dog and trees are extended, too.

7. Find the phrases that describe what the dog and the trees are thinking. Using your own words, describe what they think.

When the images are brought together again in the last stanza, they have a much deeper meaning. Your mental pictures are different from those formed at the beginning of the poem.

8. How does the image in the first stanza differ from the image in the last stanza?

Images in a Lyric Poem

"Black Hawk" and "Not Seeing Is Believing" are <u>lyric poems</u>—poems that have a single speaker and express a deeply felt thought or emotion. The speaker does not have a specific audience; that is, it seems as though the speaker is addressing himself or herself.

In William Wordsworth's lyric poem "Daffodils," the speaker is recalling an emotional moment from his past. He is recapturing a moment, making an experience become an image that he will be able to recall for the rest of his life. Wordsworth creates a strong, descriptive image: a field of daffodils. He built the overall picture by using several smaller pictures. Wordsworth appeals to your visual sense by describing the daffodils as dancers and as stars. By describing the golden flowers as "fluttering and dancing in the breeze," Wordsworth appeals to your sense of touch—you can feel the spring breeze.

9. *Look at the description of the daffodils in the rest of the poem. List at least three ways in which the poet shows the daffodils. How do his descriptions help you see the scene?*

10. *The daffodils have clearly given the poet pleasure. Explain what the poet means in these lines:*

> They flash upon that inward eye
> Which is the bliss of solitude;

Images in a Sonnet

Most of the images you have experienced so far were visual. Images, as you learned, can appeal to any of the five senses. In "On the Grasshopper and Cricket," the images involve sound and touch as well as sight.

11. *Review the poem carefully. What are the two images that appeal to your sense of hearing? What visual image is related to each?*

The sense of touch is stimulated through the images of summer and winter. In the summer the birds "are faint with the hot sun." You can almost feel the rays of heat penetrating their feathers. The birds "hide in cooling trees." You can feel the refreshing coolness in that image.

12. *What other image in this poem appeals to the sense of touch?*

"On the Grasshopper and Cricket" is a kind of poem called a sonnet— a fourteen-line lyric poem with a fixed pattern of rhyme and meter.

Usually the lines in a sonnet are in iambic pentameter (in which each line consists of five iambic feet).

Sonnets originated in Italy in the 1200s. They were a popular poetic form in England before the time of Shakespeare. No other form of poetry has been in regular use for so long or has been used by so many different poets.

"On the Grasshopper and Cricket" is an example of the Italian form of the sonnet. It falls into two main parts: the first part is eight lines long, the second is six lines. In the Italian sonnet the first part often discusses the poet's theme—the underlying message, or central idea of the poem. In the second part the poet responds to or comments on the theme. The two parts of an Italian sonnet can also deal with two related topics.

In Keats's sonnet "On the Grasshopper and Cricket," something the poet hears in winter reminds him of a sound heard in summer. The two parts of the sonnet bring together the feelings and impressions of the two seasons.

The rhyme scheme of sonnets can vary. Keats's poem uses a pattern commonly found in sonnets. The first eight lines are rhymed *abba abba.* The last six lines are rhymed *cde cde.*

Look closely at the first part of the poem. Notice that the first line, which ends in *dead,* doesn't really rhyme with the lines ending in *mead, lead,* and *weed.* There are two possible explanations for this. One is that Keats was writing almost two hundred years ago and the word *dead* may have been pronounced differently. The second possibility is that Keats was using eye rhyme. That is, he was treating words that look alike as if they rhymed, even though they do not sound alike.

13. Think of at least two pairs of words that would create eye rhyme.

Questions for Thought and Discussion

The questions and activities that follow will help you explore the four poems in this chapter in more depth and at the same time develop your critical thinking skills.

1. **Comparing.** Compare the attitudes toward nature in "Daffodils," "On

the Grasshopper and Cricket," and "Illinois: At Night, Black Hawk's Statue Broods." What similarities and differences can you find?

2. **Inferring.** Why do you think Paul Petrie gave his poem the title "Not Seeing Is Believing"? What images in the poem might be related to the title?

3. **Synthesizing.** What do you think is the purpose of each part of "On the Grasshopper and Cricket"? How are the two parts connected?

4. **Analyzing Rhyme Scheme.** What is the rhyme scheme of "Daffodils"? Choose one stanza and explain what words the rhyme scheme emphasizes.

Writing About Literature

Several suggestions for writing projects are given below. You may be asked to complete one or more of these projects. If you have any questions about how to begin a writing assignment, review Using the Writing Process, beginning on page 249.

1. **Analyzing an Image.** Select any one image from the poems in this chapter. Write a paragraph or two telling what associations the image has for you. Explain why you think it is an effective or an ineffective image.

2. **Describing a Place.** Imagine that you have been turned into a statue. Your statue has been set up somewhere in or near your school. Write a paragraph or two describing what you see. Try to create specific images to express your feelings about what you see.

3. **Creating a Class Poem.** Choose a place near your school to observe a passing scene. Make a list of the things that you see. Then select the one item on your list that you think tells the most about the school scene. Compare your image with the images of other students. What does each image tell about the area around your school? Finally, as a class, use everyone's image to make a poem about the neighborhood around your school. Arrange the images in the order that you think is most effective.

Selections	*Dream Deferred*
	LANGSTON HUGHES

Martin Luther King Jr.
GWENDOLYN BROOKS

A Red, Red Rose
ROBERT BURNS

Lesson   *Figurative Language*

❖

About the Selections

In this chapter you will read three poems. Two were composed by black Americans during the twentieth century. The third poem was written by a Scottish poet in the late 1700s. All three poets use imagery and language to make their ideas and emotions more vivid.

Langston Hughes (1902–1967) is one of the greatest black American writers of this century. Born in Joplin, Missouri, he grew up in Kansas. After graduating from high school, he spent several years traveling and working at odd jobs.

When Hughes was working in a hotel in Washington, D.C., he noticed the poet Vachel Lindsay eating in the hotel restaurant. Hughes gave Lindsay some of his poetry to read. Lindsay liked the young man's work so much that he helped Hughes get his poetry published.

In 1926 Hughes's first book of poetry, *The Weary Blues*, was published. The success of the book helped him get a scholarship that enabled him to attend college. After college, Hughes traveled and visited many parts of the world. At the same time, he continued to write plays, novels, stories, and poetry. Hughes's work focused on the despair of blacks unable to escape their economic and social conditions.

The second poem, "Martin Luther King Jr.," is a tribute to the well-known civil rights leader of the 1950s and 1960s. A tribute is something done as a mark of respect or admiration for a person. After the assassination of Martin Luther King, Jr., in 1968, many speeches, books, and poems were written about King and his commitment to peace, non-violence, and the equality of all people. Gwendolyn Brooks's short poem is an effective tribute to King.

Gwendolyn Brooks was born in Topeka, Kansas, in 1917, but she grew up in Chicago and still lives there. At twenty-eight, her first volume of poetry was published. In 1950 Gwendolyn Brooks won the Pulitzer Prize for her book of poetry *Annie Allen*. In 1969 she was named poet laureate, or official poet, of the state of Illinois.

Readers often comment on the startling imagery in Brooks's poetry. She does not let either anger or sentimentality get in the way of her remarkably clear-sighted view of life.

"A Red, Red Rose" by Robert Burns will take you back in time and place to the late 1700s in Scotland. Although the language is slightly different from modern English, the poem is easy to read. Its theme is simple and direct. It is the message of enduring love.

Robert Burns was born to a poor Scottish farm family in 1759. His father taught him to read, but young Robert had little formal schooling. His mother taught him many old Scottish songs and folktales. These greatly influenced his writing.

After his father's death, Burns continued to farm, but he did not do well. Discouraged, he decided to settle in Jamaica in the West Indies. To raise money for the journey, he published a book of his poems. The book became an instant success. Burns gave up the idea of leaving Scotland, married, and eventually settled back into farming again. He continued to write poetry, but gradually his health began to fail. He died in 1796 at the age of thirty-seven.

Burns's best poetry uses Scottish dialect. <u>Dialect</u> is the expressions and pronunciations that are unique to people of a certain group or of a particular region. Burns wrote poems that are full of warmth and good humor.

However, he is best remembered for the hundreds of songs he wrote. Many are original Scottish tunes. Others are based on old Scottish songs.

Many of Burns's songs, including "A Red, Red Rose," are love songs. Others are patriotic songs about great events in Scottish history. Burns also wrote songs about friendship and "Auld Lang Syne" is probably his best-known work outside Scotland.

Lesson Preview

The lesson that follows the three poems focuses on <u>figurative language</u>—words and phrases used in unusual ways to create strong, vivid images, to focus attention on certain ideas, and to compare things that are basically different. When words or phrases are used figuratively, they have meanings other than their usual, or literal, meanings.

Figurative language makes use of <u>figures of speech</u>—words or phrases that create vivid images by contrasting different, or dissimilar, things. A figure of speech has meaning other than its ordinary meaning. As you will read, there are different kinds of figures of speech. Although you may not be aware of it, you use figurative language in everyday conversation. You sometimes hear people say, for example, "We were dead tired." They do not mean that they were actually dead, but that they were extremely tired. The phrase "dead tired" creates an image of just *how* tired they were.

The questions that follow will help you understand how the poets used figurative language in the poems you are about to read. As you read, think about how you would answer these questions.

1 To what does the phrase "Dream Deferred" refer? What comparisons is Langston Hughes making in the poem?

2 "Martin Luther King Jr." contains several strong images. What does each image say about King? What kind of comparison is involved in each?

3 What comparison does Robert Burns make in "A Red, Red Rose"? What images do those comparisons create? How do you think the images add to the poem?

Vocabulary

Here are some difficult words that appear in the poems that follow. Study the words and their definitions, as well as the sentences that show how the words are used. This will help you get the most from your reading.

deferred put off; postponed. *Because of the heavy snowstorm predicted for the weekend, Sue deferred her trip until the following week.*

fester to rot; to cause increasing poisoning or irritation. *The boy did not clean his cut with an antiseptic and it soon began to fester.*

anoint to rub with a healing oil. *During the service of baptism, the priest will anoint the child.*

barricades barriers; obstacles. *In order to keep the baby from falling, George and Sue made barricades in front of both stairways.*

Dream Deferred

LANGSTON HUGHES

What happens to a dream deferred?

    Does it dry up
    like a raisin in the sun?
    Or fester like a sore—
5   And then run?
    Does it stink like rotten meat?
    Or crust and sugar over—
    like a syrupy sweet?

    Maybe it just sags
10   like a heavy load.

*   Or does it explode?*

Martin Luther King Jr.

GWENDOLYN BROOKS

A man went forth with gifts.

He was a prose poem.[1]
He was a tragic grace.
He was a warm music.

---

1. prose poem: a brief, intense passage
that is printed as prose in complete lines
but contains elements of poetry such as
rhythm, rhyme, figures of speech, alliteration, and vivid images.

5 He tried to heal the vivid volcanoes.
His ashes are
    reading the world.

His Dream still wishes to anoint
    the barricades of faith and of control.

10 His word still burns the center of the sun,
    above the thousands and the
    hundred thousands.

The word was Justice. It was spoken.

So it shall be spoken.
15 So it shall be done.

A Red, Red Rose

ROBERT BURNS

My love is like a red, red rose
    That's newly sprung in June:
My love is like the melody
    That's sweetly played in tune.

5 As fair art thou, my bonnie lass,
    So deep in love am I:
And I will love thee still, my dear,
    Till a' the seas gang dry.

Till a' the seas gang dry, my dear,
10   And the rocks melt wi' the sun:
And I will love thee still, my dear,
    While the sands o' life shall run.

And fare thee weel, my only love,
    And fare thee weel a while!
15   And I will come again, my love,
    Thou' it were ten thousand mile.

Reviewing the Selections

Answer each of the following questions. You may look back at the poems if necessary.

Recalling Facts

1. In "A Red, Red Rose" the speaker promises that he will be in love
   □ a. until spring is over.
   □ b. for eternity.
   □ c. until he returns from overseas.
   □ d. as long as the oceans sound like music.

Understanding Main Ideas

2. According to the poem "Martin Luther King Jr.," King's ideas
   □ a. are no longer heard today.
   □ b. were more like poetry than prose.
   □ c. caused volcanoes to erupt.
   □ d. continue to be important.

Placing Events in Order

3. In "Martin Luther King Jr." justice
   □ a. is something that people talk about but never get.
   □ b. was spoken of by Martin Luther King, Jr., and will be achieved in the future.
   □ c. will never be more than a dream.
   □ d. has gone and will never return.

Finding Supporting Details

4. In "Dream Deferred" what does the narrator suggest will happen to an unfulfilled dream?
   □ a. It will become explosive.
   □ b. It will disappear.
   □ c. It will help feed a person's soul.
   □ d. It will make a person ambitious.

5. "Till <u>a' the seas gang dry.</u>" In this context
   a' the seas gang dry means
   - ☐ a. the seas will never go dry.
   - ☐ b. below the seas everything is dry.
   - ☐ c. all the seas go dry.
   - ☐ d. all the seas are joined into one.

Interpreting the Selections

Answer each of the following questions. You may look back at the poems
if necessary.

6. The poem "Martin Luther King Jr." implies
   that King
   - ☐ a. had completed what he set out to do
     in life.
   - ☐ b. made efforts that were largely
     unsuccessful.
   - ☐ c. began something that is still being
     carried on.
   - ☐ d. should have been more careful.

7. In Langston Hughes's poem, the lines "Maybe
   it just sags / like a heavy load" suggest that a
   dream deferred
   - ☐ a. will always fall short of reality.
   - ☐ b. becomes a heavy weight.
   - ☐ c. is an easy burden to shoulder.
   - ☐ d. is not easy for a weak person to carry.

8. One of Langston Hughes's purposes in writing "Dream Deferred" was probably to
   - ☐ a. issue a warning.
   - ☐ b. write a song.
   - ☐ c. entertain the reader.
   - ☐ d. help people understand their dreams.

9. "Dream Deferred" is different from the other two poems in that it
   - ☐ a. is longer.
   - ☐ b. is serious.
   - ☐ c. has no lines that rhyme.
   - ☐ d. asks questions.

10. In the last stanza of "A Red, Red Rose," the speaker in the poem is
    - ☐ a. worried that the girl doesn't love him.
    - ☐ b. saying good-bye.
    - ☐ c. proposing marriage.
    - ☐ d. returning from a long voyage.

Figurative Language

Poetry, like other forms of literature, makes use of figurative language. Writers constantly experiment with language, using words and phrases in new and unusual ways to emphasize ideas, to create humor, to make comparisons, and to develop fresh images. Poets often build images by making comparisons. Comparisons help you to see what the poet is describing in new ways.

Figures of speech are comparisons in which the writer uses words and phrases to add vividness and interest or to achieve special effects and meanings. The words and phrases in a figure of speech have meanings outside their ordinary meanings.

For example, in the sentence, "George is like a bear in the morning," the comparison suggests that George, like a bear, is cross and easily angered. When you compare George and the bear, you get a strong visual image of George's behavior. Such a comparison is called a simile. *Simile* is related to the word *similar.* A <u>simile</u> is a direct comparison between two unlike things that are connected by the word *like, as,* or *resembles,* or the verb *appears* or *seems.* The purpose of a simile is to give you a vivid new way of looking at one of the things.

Another figure of speech is the metaphor. As you learned in Chapter 2, a metaphor is an implied comparison between two unlike, or dissimilar, things. It does not use the word *like, as,* or *resembles.* For example, in the sentence, "Her heart is stone," *heart* and *stone* are compared. You know that those words have very different literal meanings. Yet you assign the qualities of a stone—its appearance, hardness, coldness—to the woman's heart, or feelings. You understand the comparison because you are aware of the connotations of the word *stone.*

Figurative language is important in poetry because it forces you to notice the connotations (suggestions) rather than the denotations (literal meanings) of words. Using a minimum of words, a poet can create a powerful, intense image. Figurative language is made up of many different figures of speech. In this lesson you will study a few of the basic figures found in poetry.

Similes in "Dream Deferred"

"Dream Deferred" is a short poem. It consists almost entirely of rhetorical questions. A rhetorical question is asked only for dramatic effect and not to seek an answer. The first line contains the poem's main theme: "What happens to a dream deferred?"

1. What does the phrase "a dream deferred" mean?

The poet suggests possible answers to the main question by posing other questions. Look closely at the rhetorical questions. The first two ask:

> Does it dry up
> like a raisin in the sun?
>
> Or fester like a sore—
> And then run?

In each of those questions the dream is compared to something. It is compared to a raisin that has dried up in the sun and then to a sore that festers and runs. Both comparisons are similes because two unlike things are being compared, and they are joined by the word *like.*

Think about the images created by those similes. Remember that they are answering the rhetorical question, "What happens to a dream deferred?" The first simile creates an image of a raisin, plump and sweet, slowly drying in the sun. The raisin, left in the sun, will continue to dry out and shrivel. A dream, by contrast, is usually hopeful and full of life. The second simile creates a picture of a festering, oozing sore. The image suggests that a dream deferred decays and the infection spreads.

2. There are three other similes in "Dream Deferred." What are they? What picture does each create in your mind? What does each image say about a dream that is deferred?

In the last line of the poem, a final question is posed as a possible answer to the main rhetorical question. The final question is different from the earlier questions in two ways.

3. What are two ways in which the final question differs from the earlier ones? What effect do those differences have on the last question? On the poem as a whole?

In "Dream Deferred" Hughes describes the frustration and despair of never realizing a dream, of continually waiting for social and economic conditions to change. In the poem you can sense Hughes's tone—a writer's attitude toward his or her subject, audience, or self. A poet creates a tone through his or her choice of words, details, and images.

4. What is the poet's tone in "Dream Deferred"? Cite evidence from the poem to support your conclusion.

Metaphors in "Martin Luther King Jr."

In "Martin Luther King Jr." Brooks creates powerful images by using metaphors. Look at lines 2, 3, and 4. If similes had been used instead of metaphors, the lines would have read:

> He was like a prose poem.
> He was like a tragic grace.
> He was like a warm music.

Notice the difference, however, between those lines and the actual lines in the poem. Brooks creates a particular image of Martin Luther King, Jr., by stating that he *was* each of those things. The metaphors tell you something about the kind of person Martin Luther King, Jr., was.

In a simile A *is like* B. In a metaphor A *is* B. Two terms that are not at all alike are compared to each other. Look again at the metaphor in line 2. Brooks calls Martin Luther King, Jr., a prose poem. As you read in the footnote, a prose poem is an unusual literary form that combines elements of prose and poetry. By comparing King to a prose poem, Brooks is suggesting King's unusual combination of qualities. The word *poem* suggests that he possessed musical sounds and rhythm as well as rich imagery. *Prose* suggests earthiness, a connection with the common people and their concerns. Thus, a *prose poem* suggests King was both a visionary and an effective popular leader.

5. What are the metaphors in lines 3 and 4 of "Martin Luther King Jr."? What does each metaphor tell you about Martin Luther King? Write several characteristics that each metaphor suggests.

Implicit Metaphors

The metaphors that you have seen so far suggest that one thing is another, A *is* B. Metaphors can also be implicit. An implicit metaphor occurs when one of the terms is not stated but suggested by the context. For example, a child might be described as "galloping" across a yard. Galloping is something that horses do, not people. Behind the description is an implicit, or unstated, metaphor: the child moves with the lively quickness of a horse. An adult might be described as "drifting" into a room. Snow and balloons drift. Here again, the metaphor is implicit: the person has the lightness of a balloon, or maybe a snowflake, and moves without a destination in mind.

Gwendolyn Brooks's poem has both stated and implicit metaphors. Look at line 5 of "Martin Luther King Jr." There are two metaphors in that line. The first implicit metaphor is implied by the verb *heal.*

In our society you probably think of healers as doctors, nurses, dentists, veterinarians, and other medical people. But people without medical training can also help to heal. For example, friends or parents can help to heal hurt feelings. Some people believe in miracle workers. Perhaps you can think of still other examples of healers. Any or all of these possibilities are implied here by the verb *heal.*

The second metaphor in line 5 is contained in the phrase "vivid volcanoes." Martin Luther King, Jr., tried to calm explosive and life-threatening conditions in the world—the conditions that lead to fighting, division, and hatred. Those conditions are the "vivid volcanoes."

6. Identify another metaphor or implicit metaphor in the poem. What images does the metaphor suggest? How does the metaphor affect the way that you see Martin Luther King, Jr.?

Figurative Language in "A Red, Red Rose"

The last poem is a love song. It is written in quatrains. A <u>quatrain</u> is a four-line stanza, a very common form in English poetry.

In "A Red, Red Rose" the first quatrain contains two similes. Each contributes to the mood, or feeling, of the poem.

7. Reread the first quatrain. Identify each simile. What mood do the similes help to create?

In the second stanza, the speaker introduces a simile with the word *as.*

> As fair thou art, my bonnie lass,
> So deep in love am I:

That simile is a bit complicated because the poet has reversed the usual order of the comparison. If you were writing the simile in everyday language and order, you would say, "My bonnie lass, I am so deep in love as you are fair."

8. What ideas or feelings does the previous simile emphasize?

In "A Red, Red Rose" Burns uses another figure of speech when he deliberately exaggerates to emphasize an idea or a feeling. This kind of exaggeration is called <u>hyperbole</u>. You hear hyperbole often in everyday conversation. You probably have heard someone say, "The movie scared us to death." The people did not actually die from fear, although they were very frightened.

9. In stanzas 3 and 4 of "A Red, Red Rose," what examples of hyperbole do you find? What image does each create?

Dialect

Like many of Robert Burns's poems, "A Red, Red Rose" is written in a Scottish dialect. As you have read, dialect is the pattern of speech used by people of a certain group or of a particular region. A dialect involves differences in pronunciation and vocabulary. In this poem the differences in vocabulary are the Scottish expressions *bonnie, lass,* and *gang* (for *go*).

The grammar of a dialect differs in some ways from the standard grammar of the parent language. For example, Burns uses the word *mile* instead of *miles.* Also, some pronunciations within a dialect are different. If this poem were read aloud by a Scottish person, most words would sound different than if it were read by an American. The poet indicates several pronunciations by writing the words as they sound: *a', wi', weel, Thou',* for *all, with, well,* and *though.*

10. If "A Red, Red Rose" were written completely in Scottish dialect, it would probably look very different. Why do you think Burns chose to write the poem only partly in dialect?

Questions for Thought and Discussion

The questions and activities that follow will help you explore the three poems in this chapter in more depth and at the same time develop your critical thinking skills.

1. **Taking a Stand.** In "Dream Deferred" which answer to the question "What happens to a dream deferred?" do you think is most true? Give reasons for your answer.

2. **Comparing.** Compare the meaning of the last line of "Dream Deferred" to the "vivid volcanoes" of "Martin Luther King Jr."

3. **Interpreting.** How long does the speaker in "A Red, Red Rose" say that his love will last? Does he really mean that? If not, what do you think he does mean?

4. **Using Metaphors.** Divide the class into small groups. Each group should choose a well-known leader such as Martin Luther King, Jr. Make a list of the qualities you associate with that person. Then think of at least four metaphors to describe those qualities. Use the metaphors in Gwendolyn Brooks's poem as a model.

Writing About Literature

Several suggestions for writing projects are given below. You may be asked to complete one or more of these projects. If you have any questions about how to begin a writing assignment, review Using the Writing Process, beginning on page 249.

1. **Creating a Poem.** Imagine that you had a dream that you very much wanted to come true. Then write a short poem modeled on "Dream Deferred" but entitle your poem "Dream Fulfilled." Create images using either similes or metaphors in your poem.

2. **Analyzing a Character.** Gwendolyn Brooks's poem is a tribute to Martin Luther King, Jr. Think of someone you know and admire. The person might or might not be famous. Write a brief description of the person, using figurative language. Your description can be in prose or poetry, but it should capture some essential characteristics of the person.

Figurative Language

3. **Writing in Dialect.** You have no doubt heard different regional accents of English. Americans in the southern United States speak differently from New Englanders or Midwesterners. British people sound different from Americans, and Australians and Canadians have their own pronunciations and expressions. Even people from a nearby town may seem to speak in a different dialect because of the way they pronounce certain words. Write a paragraph about a feeling such as anger, happiness, or love using a particular dialect. To do this, use spellings that reflect the pronunciations in the dialect, as well as words and expressions that are special to that dialect.

Chapter 6

Selections

O Captain! My Captain!
WALT WHITMAN

The Train
EMILY DICKINSON

The Noise That Time Makes
MERRILL MOORE

Lesson   *Special Kinds of Metaphors*

❖

About the Selections

The first poem, "O Captain! My Captain!", was written by Walt Whitman (1819–1892) just after the American Civil War ended. Two tragedies, the nation's recent battles and the death of President Abraham Lincoln, are woven into the poem.

From 1861 to 1865 the United States was torn apart by the Civil War. It was a conflict between regions and ideologies. The South wanted to form a separate, slaveholding nation called the Confederate States of America. The North wanted to preserve the Union—part slave, part free—as one nation, the United States.

The war was the bloodiest struggle the world had known up to that time. It remains the costliest war, in terms of lives lost, in American history. There was hardly an American family that was not directly affected by the war.

The president of the United States during the Civil War was Abraham Lincoln. Among Lincoln's greatest admirers was Walt Whitman.

Whitman was born on Long Island, New York, and grew up in

Brooklyn. As a young man, he learned the printing trade and also became a newspaper reporter. He was firmly against slavery.

In 1855 Whitman published a little volume of his own poetry called *Leaves of Grass*. During the next thirty-five years he periodically reprinted the volume, each time adding more poems. By the time Whitman died in 1892, the book had been revised nine times.

Leaves of Grass surprised many people. Unlike most poetry of the time, many of Whitman's poems were written in free verse. His poems celebrated the relationship between humanity and nature. They often dealt with the beauty of America and of American ideals.

The Civil War brought Whitman to Washington, D.C., to care for a brother and other soldiers who had been wounded in the fighting. After his brother recovered, Whitman stayed on in Washington. He earned his living working in a government office. He spent his spare time helping wounded soldiers, both Union and Confederate, who were housed in military hospitals near the capital. He also wrote poetry about the war and its battles.

In April 1865 the Confederacy surrendered and the war ended. Led by Lincoln, the Union had triumphed, and the United States was reunited as one country.

Just five days after the surrender, however, President Lincoln was shot as he watched a play at Ford's Theater in Washington. Whitman was devastated. "O Captain! My Captain!" describes his feelings about the death of President Lincoln.

Emily Dickinson (1830–1886), author of "The Train," was born in Amherst, Massachusetts. Except for a year at college, she spent her entire life in Amherst. Dickinson continued her adult life in the house where she was brought up, and as she grew older, she rarely left the house or its garden.

Unlike the flamboyant Whitman, Emily Dickinson was a very private poet. She wrote more than 1,700 poems, yet she wanted none of them to be published. A few friends were occasionally allowed glimpses of selected poems, but the majority of her work was not read until after her death.

Dickinson's poems are short, and her style is plain and spare.

Yet even though her world was small and her experiences limited, Dickinson still used her poetry to explore questions about faith, love, death, and nature. Today literary critics consider her to be one of America's greatest poets.

The author of the third poem, Merrill Moore, was born in 1903 in Columbia, Tennessee. He grew up in Nashville and attended Vanderbilt University. At the university he met a number of well-known poets.

Like William Carlos Williams, whose poem "View of a Lake" you read earlier, Merrill Moore pursued a medical career. He eventually settled in Boston, where he practiced psychiatry and taught at Harvard Medical School.

Moore wrote poetry all his life. "I am most interested in human personality and its problems," he wrote, "and it is on that common interest in my own life that medicine and poetry meet." Most of his poems, including "The Noise That Time Makes," are sonnets. He sometimes wrote four or five sonnets a day. He seldom revised a poem, preferring instead to move on to a new one. Because he wrote so quickly, his sonnets vary in quality. However, the one that you will read stands among his best.

Lesson Preview

The lesson that follows the three poems deals with special kinds of metaphors. The metaphors in the poems that you will read here are developed more fully than those in the poems in Chapter 5. The questions below will help you identify the different kinds of metaphors. As you read, think about how you would answer these questions.

1 Look for one main metaphor in each poem. What is it?

2 In "O Captain! My Captain!" what do you think the captain, the ship, and the port stand for?

3 In "The Train," notice the different activities of the train. What is the train doing at each point in the poem?

4 In "The Noise That Time Makes," what sort of noise does time make? What examples does the poet give?

Vocabulary

Here are some difficult words that appear in the poems that follow. Study the words and their definitions, as well as the sentences that show how the words are used. This will help you get the most from your reading.

keel the center beam or plate that runs along the lowest part of the bottom of a ship. *We took the boat out of the water in order to make repairs to the keel.*

prodigious very great; huge. *George will gain weight if he keeps eating such prodigious amounts of food.*

supercilious proud and scornful; haughty. *The other students did not know that Sue's supercilious silence was only a disguise for her shyness.*

quarry a place where stone, marble, or slate is cut out of the earth. *The artist went to the quarry to select the perfect piece of marble for his sculpture.*

O Captain! My Captain!

WALT WHITMAN

O Captain! my Captain! our fearful trip is done,
The ship has weather'd every rack, the prize we sought is won,
The port is near, the bells I hear, the people all exulting,
While follow eyes the steady keel, the vessel grim and daring;
5   But O heart! heart! heart!
           O the bleeding drops of red,
             Where on the deck my Captain lies,
              Fallen cold and dead.

O Captain! my Captain! rise up and hear the bells;
10 Rise up—for you the flag is flung—for you the bugle trills,
For you bouquets and ribbon'd wreaths—for you the shores a-crowding,
For you they call, the swaying mass, their eager faces turning;
        Here Captain! dear father!
          This arm beneath your head!
15   It is some dream that on the deck,
             You've fallen cold and dead.

My Captain does not answer, his lips are pale and still,
My father does not feel my arm, he has no pulse nor will,
The ship is anchor'd safe and sound, its voyage closed and done,
20 From fearful trip the victor ship comes in with object won;

        Exault O shores, and ring O bells!
         But I with mournful tread,
           Walk the deck my Captain lies,
            Fallen cold and dead.

        Special Kinds of Metaphors

The Train

EMILY DICKINSON

I like to see it lap the miles,
And lick the valleys up,
And stop to feed itself at tanks;
And then, prodigious, step

5　Around a pile of mountains,
And, supercilious, peer
In shanties by the sides of roads;
And then a quarry pare[1]

To fit its sides, and crawl between,
10　Complaining all the while
In horrid, hooting stanza;
Then chase itself down hill

And neigh like Boanerges;[2]
Then, punctual as a star,
15　Stop—docile and omnipotent—[3]
At its own stable door.

---

1. pare: trim or cut away. **2. Boanerges (boh-AH-ner-jeez):** A Hebrew expression meaning the sons of thunder. Jesus gave the apostles John and James the name Boanerges. **3. docile and omnipotent:** tame and all-powerful.

The Noise That Time Makes

MERRILL MOORE

The noise that Time makes in passing by
Is very slight but even you can hear it,
Having not necessarily to be near it,
Needing only the slightest will to try:

5 Hold the receiver of a telephone
To your ear when no one is talking on the line,
And what may at first sound to you like the whine
Of wind over distant wires is Time's own
Garments brushing against a windy cloud.

10 That same noise again, but not so well,
May be heard by taking a small cockle-shell
From the sand and holding it against your head;

Then you can hear Time's footsteps as they pass
Over the earth brushing the eternal grass.

Reviewing the Selections

Answer each of the following questions. You may look back at the poems if necessary.

Recalling Facts

1. The captain of "O Captain! My Captain!" is captain of
   ☐ a. a football team.
   ☐ b. an army unit.
   ☐ c. a ship.
   ☐ d. a military squad.

Understanding Main Ideas

2. In "The Train" the poet writes about the train as if it were
   ☐ a. an animal.
   ☐ b. a ship.
   ☐ c. a person.
   ☐ d. a thunderstorm.

Placing Events in Order

3. In "The Train" the train neighs just before it
   ☐ a. laps the miles.
   ☐ b. steps around a pile of mountains.
   ☐ c. chases itself downhill.
   ☐ d. stops.

Finding Supporting Details

4. In "The Noise That Time Makes," what does the speaker suggest be held against the head?
   ☐ a. a small cockle-shell
   ☐ b. a sand dollar
   ☐ c. a piece of driftwood
   ☐ d. a bottle with a message in it

5. "But I with mournful <u>tread</u>, / Walk the deck
   my Captain lies, / Fallen cold and dead." In
   this context *tread* means
   □ a. face.
   □ b. fear.
   □ c. burdens.
   □ d. steps.

Interpreting the Selections

Answer each of the following questions. You may look back at the poems
if necessary.

6. In "The Train" the "horrid, hooting stanza" is
   □ a. an owl disturbed by the train.
   □ b. a loud poem.
   □ c. the train's whistle.
   □ d. the sound of a train crash.

7. In "The Noise That Time Makes," the phrase
   "Time's own garments" suggests that the poet
   thinks of time as
   □ a. an animal.
   □ b. a flower.
   □ c. a person.
   □ d. the ocean.

8. In "O Captain! My Captain!" the author's
   purpose is to
   ☐ a. express how he feels about his
      captain's death.
   ☐ b. condemn those who caused the
      captain's death.
   ☐ c. tell about the captain's many victories.
   ☐ d. describe his joy at reaching a safe port.

9. Think about "The Train" and "The Noise That
   Time Makes." A train is the subject of one
   poem, and time is the subject of the other. In
   each poem the subject
   ☐ a. makes the poet feel sad.
   ☐ b. is discussed in scientific terms.
   ☐ c. is treated as if it were a living thing.
   ☐ d. is one that few people have
      experience with.

10. In "The Noise That Time Makes," the noise is
    ☐ a. very soft.
    ☐ b. steady, like a ticking clock.
    ☐ c. loud and crashing.
    ☐ d. unpleasant and jarring.

Special Kinds of Metaphors

In Chapter 5 you examined several figures of speech, including metaphors. The metaphors in "Martin Luther King Jr." were fairly simple and straightforward. As you will recall, some implied comparisons were stated directly: "He was a prose poem"; while others were implicit metaphors: "He tried to heal. . . ." In each case, Gwendolyn Brooks expresses her thought through the metaphor and then moves on to another, very different image.

By contrast, in the first two poems you have just read, the poets create <u>extended metaphors</u>. That is, the poets introduce a basic, or main, metaphor involving the entire poem, and the shorter metaphors within the poem contribute directly to the main metaphor. In an extended metaphor, the poet makes many links between the two unlike things being compared. The result is a strong and lasting image.

Reading "O Captain! My Captain!"

As you have already seen, poetry is concentrated. In just a few words or lines, a poet conveys a great deal of information, as well as a variety of feelings. The first four lines of Walt Whitman's famous poem provide a remarkable amount of information. They also establish the mood, or atmosphere.

Look at the first line: "O Captain! My Captain! our fearful trip is done." The first words introduce the subject of the poem. The poem's speaker is addressing the captain directly. This kind of metaphor is called apostrophe—the poet formally addresses a thing or an absent person as though that thing or person is present. In the second phrase, the word *my* explains the relationship between the speaker and the captain. The speaker is under the captain's command. He is, therefore, an officer or a sailor on the ship.

The word *my* also suggests the speaker's feelings toward the captain. He feels loyalty, respect, and admiration. Later in the poem, you learn that he loves the captain like a father. In the next phrase, "our fearful trip is done," the speaker reveals that the ship is returning from a dangerous and frightening voyage.

1. Read the first line carefully. What mood do you think it establishes?

The second line adds more detail: "The ship has weather'd every rack, the prize we sought is won." Despite dangers and difficulties, the ship is returning in one piece. The captain has achieved his purpose. In lines 3 and 4, you learn that the ship is entering the harbor. The people on shore are celebrating its successful return.

Changes in Mood. Suddenly, the poem changes. You learn that the captain has died:

> But O heart! heart! heart!
> O the bleeding drops of red,
> Where on the deck my Captain lies,
> Fallen cold and dead.

In fact, the captain cannot hear anything that was said to him in the first four lines of the poem. He is lying dead on the deck of the ship. Evidently, the captain's death is very recent, for the speaker has not yet really accepted it.

In the second stanza the speaker urges the captain to get up and take note of the celebrations in his honor. The speaker even tries to help the captain up.

2. What feeling does the poet create in this stanza?

Apostrophe. Apostrophe gives dramatic emphasis to a poet's thoughts by making the object vividly real. By addressing Lincoln as though he were still alive, Whitman adds drama and imagery to the poem. He refers to Lincoln as "captain" and to the government as a "ship." Whitman gives you concrete terms, *captain* and *ship*, to create a stronger image in your mind.

   3. Reread the poem using "Lincoln" for "Captain" and "government" for "ship." How do the images in the poem change?

The Extended Metaphor. "O Captain! My Captain!" is a sad, moving poem even if you do not understand the metaphors. Someone who knows nothing about Abraham Lincoln and the Civil War can read the poem and appreciate its tragic quality, simply as a poem about a captain who died after leading his ship on a difficult voyage. We know, however, that Whitman was writing a tribute to Abraham Lincoln, and that the poem is made up of a series of related metaphors.

   One implicit metaphor is the comparison between the Union, or the United States of America, and a ship. Think about what the Union had just experienced to understand the rest of the metaphor.

   4. What is the "fearful trip"? Who are the "people all exulting"? What is the "object won"?

   Taken together, those metaphors create a powerful image. Like a fearless sea captain, Abraham Lincoln has led the nation through fierce seas. Just as the ship is reaching a safe harbor, however, its captain is killed. He cannot enjoy the rewards of peace, the cheers of the crowds. All the individual metaphors—the storm, the ship, the captain—are related. They combine to create a single image—the death of a president who has struggled to hold the country together. That is an extended metaphor.

Implicit Metaphors

In "The Train" Emily Dickinson uses an extended metaphor in which she compares a train to an animal. Through that metaphor, you can see how she feels about the train.

The basic, or main, metaphor in this poem is implicit. The poet does not mention the word *train* in the poem. The extended image is of a large, lively, curious animal. In the poem the animal "lap[s] the miles," "lick[s] the valleys up," and "stop[s] to feed itself at tanks." You know that lapping, licking, and feeding are things that animals do. But what kind of animal licks valleys? Because you know that the poem is about a train, you form an image of the train as a great, powerful, greedy animal.

5. Look up the verb lap *in a dictionary. What different meanings are given? Which meaning do you think Dickinson intended the word to have in line 1? Do you think she intended to suggest more than one meaning? Explain your answer.*

6. What other activities of the train does the poet describe? What animals do you associate with those activities?

Within the main metaphor of the train-as-animal, there are other metaphors. The train's whistle, for example, is a "horrid, hooting stanza." The entrance to a train's roundhouse—the building for storing and re-pairing locomotives—is "the stable door." There also are similes: "neigh like Boanerges" and "punctual as a star."

7. How do those metaphors and similes add to the overall extended metaphor of the poem?

The extended metaphor in this poem is built on a series of implicit metaphors. You will recall that in a metaphor A *is* B. In an implicit metaphor only A is mentioned and B is suggested.

9. Make up your own implicit metaphor. Think of an object that moves and the animal that you think it most closely resembles. In two or three sen-tences, and without naming the object, tell how the object moves or what it does, using words associated with the animal you think it resembles.

Personification

In "The Noise That Time Makes," Merrill Moore uses a figure of speech called personification. In <u>personification</u> an animal, object, or idea is given human qualities. When you say that the sun smiled or, as in Wordsworth's poem "Daffodils," that the daffodils were "dancing in the breeze," you are personifying those objects by speaking of them as if they were people.

Poets often use personification to describe abstract ideas such as freedom, truth, or beauty. Many painters and sculptors also have used personification to express ideas. The Statue of Liberty in New York harbor is an example: She personifies liberty.

In "The Noise That Time Makes," Moore has personified the idea of time. The poem does not state directly that time is a person. However, time is described in ways that can apply only to a person.

9. *Look at these excerpts from the poem. How does each personify time?*

    a. *And what may at first sound to you like the whine*
      Of wind over distant wires is Time's own
      Garments brushing against a windy cloud.

    b. *Then you can hear Time's footsteps as they pass*
      Over the earth brushing the eternal grass.

10. *Reread the poem, keeping in mind the personification. Do you sense it in the first part of the poem? Why?*

11. *The poet tells you two ways to hear the noise that time makes. How would you describe the noise? Why do many people fail to hear it?*

Questions for Thought and Discussion

The questions and activities that follow will help you explore the three poems in this chapter in more depth and at the same time develop your critical thinking skills.

1. **Evaluating.** Imagine that someone wrote a poem called "The Death of Abraham Lincoln." In the poem the poet listed the president's accomplishments and expressed how bad he or she felt that the president had died just as the war was won. Do you think the poem would have been as effective as "O Captain! My Captain!"? Explain your answer.

2. **Taking a Stand.** Review all three poems in the chapter and decide which poem you think has the most vivid and powerful images. Share your views and your reasons for choosing certain images with the rest of the class.

3. **Identifying the Author's Purpose.** In "The Noise That Time Makes," the poet seems to assume that people want to hear time pass. Why might the poet feel that way? What do you think people are missing if they don't stop to listen to the passage of time?

Writing About Literature

Several suggestions for writing projects are given below. You may be asked to complete one or more of these projects. If you have any questions about how to begin a writing assignment, review Using the Writing Process, beginning on page 249.

1. **Comparing.** Choose one poem from Chapter 5 and one from this chapter. Then write a few paragraphs comparing how each uses figures of speech. You can choose poems that use different figures of speech such as similes, metaphors, implicit metaphors, extended metaphors, hyperbole, animation, and personification.

2. **Creating an Extended Metaphor.** Think of any current or historical event that has involved a president of the United States. In several paragraphs, describe the event, using an extended metaphor of the United States as a ship and the president as its captain. You can add any other elements to the metaphor that you need to tell the story.

3. **Personifying an Abstract Idea.** Choose an abstract idea, such as truth, justice, freedom, happiness, despair, gloom, or treachery. Think about how you would personify that idea. What characteristics would a person embodying the idea have? How would the person look? Act? Talk? Describe each personal characteristic and tell how it relates to the abstract idea.

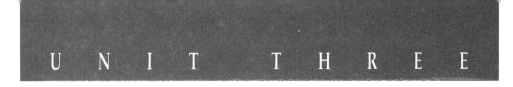

Voices in
Poetry

*I*n the first two units you read about the sounds of poetry and the images poets create. In Unit Three you will examine another element of poetry by asking yourself two important questions: Who is speaking in the poems? and To whom is the speaker talking?

Readers often assume that the person speaking in a poem is the poet, and that the poet is addressing the reader. Yet that is frequently not the case. In many poems, the speaker is not the poet but a voice that the poet has created.

To answer the question of who is speaking in a poem, think of a poem as a play. For example, suppose that you are watching a friend act in a play, and he is playing the role of a character named Chris. As you watch the play, your friend makes some ridiculous statements. Do you conclude that your friend is ridiculous, that the playwright is ridiculous, or that your friend and the playwright are trying to show something about the character Chris? You realize that your friend is speaking a character's lines and not his own thoughts.

When you watch a play, you know that the actors are playing roles. They are pretending to be people other than themselves. In reality, the actors may be like the characters they play or they may be completely different. The same is true for the playwright. Just because he or she has written the lines for the characters does not mean that the playwright agrees with what the characters say. Both the actors and the playwright, however, are interested in creating convincing characters.

When you read a poem, think of it as a short scene from a play. Try to discover who the voice in the poem belongs to and to whom that voice is speaking.

In Unit Three you will read poems that have different kinds of speakers. You will also discover that the audience—the person or thing the speaker is addressing—is important to the meaning of the poem.

Chapter 7

Selections

Factory Work
DEBORAH BOE

The River Merchant's Wife: A Letter
EZRA POUND

The Eagle That Is Forgotten
VACHEL LINDSAY

Lesson

Monologue

❖

About the Selections

Suppose that there is a shoe factory near where you live. On a class trip, you take a tour of the factory. As you walk past the machines, your guide points out a young woman who is a "shanker." The guide explains that the woman glues shanks, or metal braces, inside the bottoms of shoes. You stop to watch her. Because you look interested, the young woman tells you what she is doing.

The setting in "Factory Work," the first poem in this chapter, is a shoe factory. A young woman talks about her job in the factory. In the process, she reveals a lot about herself, too.

"Factory Work" was written by Deborah Boe. When she was three, Boe decided that she wanted to be an artist. As a teenager, she felt that she would never be a truly fine painter, so she switched her creative energies to writing poetry. Boe considers herself very lucky because the first poem she submitted for publication was accepted, and she was even paid for it! Later, however, she struggled like so many other poets to get her work published.

Boe was born in Los Angeles but spent much of her youth at her grandparents' ranch in the Mojave Desert. When she was ready for college, she chose a completely different environment, attending Bowdoin College in Maine. While she was living in Maine, Boe, like the woman in the poem, worked for a time in a shoe factory. Boe has since made her home in Massachusetts. Her first book of poems, *Mojave,* was published in 1987. She is currently working on a series of poems in which the speakers are Biblical characters such as Noah.

"Factory Work" is a poem of present-day America. The second poem, "The River Merchant's Wife: A Letter," takes you far away in both time and place. It is set in China more than twelve hundred years ago.

Once again, you hear the voice of a young woman. She is sixteen years old and has been married for two years. In keeping with Chinese custom, the marriage was arranged by the couple's families. The young people had little or nothing to say about the matter. When the girl was married at age fourteen, she barely knew her husband and was very shy. But she has grown to love him. The husband is a river merchant who travels on business. His wife misses him and is writing him a letter. The poem you will read is that letter.

Ezra Pound based his poem on one written by Li Po, a famous Chinese poet who lived from 701 to 762. Li Po's poetry was based on Chinese stories and folktales.

The poem is not a translation of Li Po's original, but rather Pound's interpretation of the Chinese original. The situation, the feelings, and the images come mainly from Li Po. However, Pound has shaped those into his own poem, using his own words and form.

Ezra Pound is one of the most important and controversial figures in American poetry. He was born in Hailey, Idaho, in 1885, and grew up in Pennsylvania. Soon after graduating from college, Pound left America for Europe. From 1908 to 1945 he lived in England, France, and Italy. During World War II Pound lived in Italy and supported the Fascist dictator Benito Mussolini. His political opinions as well as his poetry made him the center of much controversy and alienated many of his admirers.

Pound devoted his life to poetry and had strong ideas about how it should be written. He experimented with many poetic forms, and his work influenced many other poets.

Vachel Lindsay, the author of "The Eagle That Is Forgotten," was born in Springfield, Illinois, in 1879. He planned to be a minister but then studied art before finding his career in poetry.

At the age of twenty-six, Lindsay made a trip through the South, giving public readings of his poetry in exchange for room and board. Those trips inspired him to write a new kind of poetry—one intended to be performed as well as read. Some of the poems were even meant to be chanted rather than read in a regular speaking voice.

Political reform is an important theme in Lindsay's poetry. During Lindsay's time some reformers wanted better conditions for farmers. Others tried to help improve conditions for factory workers and their families. Among the reformers was John P. Altgeld, a Chicago judge. He won fame for writing a book in which he said that the poor had less than a fair chance in American life. He was among the first public officials to take up the cause of the poor. It is Altgeld who is the subject of "The Eagle That Is Forgotten."

In 1893 Altgeld was elected governor of Illinois. Shortly after he took office, he pardoned several men who had been imprisoned after the Haymarket Riot. The riot had pitted striking workers against the police and led to the arrest of a number of men accused of throwing bombs.

After studying the evidence from their trial, Altgeld pardoned the men because he believed that the trial had been unfair. However, several newspapers and many employers attacked him for releasing the prisoners. (Those attackers are the "foes" Lindsay mentions in his poem.)

Even though the newspaper attacks were unfair, they damaged Altgeld's reputation. He failed to win reelection in 1896. When he died a few years later, he was largely forgotten. Lindsay's poem assures Altgeld a place in history.

Lesson Preview

The lesson that follows the three poems focuses on the question of who is speaking in each poem. As you will learn, the speaker may or may not be the poet. Often a poet creates a character, and it is that character's voice that is heard in the poem.

The questions that follow will help you identify the speaker in each poem. As you read, think about how you would answer these questions.

1 Who is the speaker in each poem? How do you know?

2 What do you learn about the speaker in each poem?

3 Who is being addressed, or spoken to, in each poem? How do you know? How do you think the "audience" affects the way the poem is written?

Vocabulary

Here are some difficult words that appear in the poems that follow. Study the words and their definitions, as well as the sentences that show how the words are used. This will help you get the most from your reading.

eddies currents of water that move in circles against the main current. *Sometimes it is easier to catch fish in the calmer eddies than in the strong current of the stream.*

bereft deprived of. *The teacher was so surprised by George's rude remark that for a moment she was bereft of speech.*

pall a piece of heavy cloth used to cover a coffin. *Since the colonel had been a veteran of World War II, his coffin was covered with an American flag instead of a pall.*

valiant brave; courageous. *Even though our dog is smaller than the neighbors' dog, she makes a valiant attempt to protect her territory.*

zeal devotion or enthusiasm, as for a cause. *Although George was enthusiastic about repairing the car, his zeal could not disguise the fact that he knew nothing about mechanics.*

Factory Work

DEBORAH BOE

All day I stand here, like this,
over the hot-glue machine,
not too close to the wheel
that brings up the glue,
5   and I take those metal shanks,
slide the backs of them in glue
and make them lie down
on the shoe-bottoms, before the sole
goes on. It's simple, but the lasts[1]
10 weigh, give you big arms.
If I hit my boyfriend now,
in the supermarket parking lot,
he knows I hit him.

Phyllis, who stands next to me,
15 had long hair before the glue machine
got it. My machine ate up my shirt once.
I tried to get it out, the wheel
spinning on me, until someone with a brain
turned it off. It's not bad
20 here, people leave you alone,
don't ask you what you're thinking.

It's a good thing, too, because all this morning
I was remembering last night,
when I really thought my grandpa's soul

---

1. lasts: forms which are shaped like the human foot and
over which a shoe is formed.

25   had moved into the apartment,
the way the eggs fell, and the lamp
broke, like someone was trying
to communicate to me, and he
just dead this week. I wouldn't
30   blame him. That man in the next aisle
reminds me of him, a little.

It's late October now, and Eastland
needs to lay some people off.
Last week they ran a contest
35   to see which shankers shanked fastest.
I'm not embarrassed to say
I beat them all. It's all
in economy of motion, all the moves
on automatic. I almost
40   don't need to look at what
I'm doing. I'm thinking of the way
the leaves turn red when the cold
gets near them. They fall until
you're wading in red leaves up to your knees,
45   and the air snaps
in the tree-knuckles, and you begin
to see your breath rise
out of you like your own ghost
each morning you come here.

The River Merchant's Wife: A Letter

EZRA POUND

While my hair was still cut straight across my forehead
I played about the front gate, pulling flowers.
You came by on bamboo stilts, playing horse,
You walked about my seat, playing with blue plums.
5 And we went on living in the village of Chokan:
Two small people, without dislike or suspicion.

At fourteen I married My Lord you.
I never laughed, being bashful.
Lowering my head, I looked at the wall.
10 Called to, a thousand times, I never looked back.

At fifteen I stopped scowling,
I desired my dust to be mingled with yours
Forever and forever and forever.
Why should I climb the look out?

15 At sixteen you departed,
You went into far Ku-to-yen, by the river of swirling eddies,
And you have been gone five months.
The monkeys make sorrowful noise overhead.

You dragged your feet when you went out.
20 By the gate now, the moss is grown, the different mosses,
Too deep to clear them away!
The leaves fall early this autumn, in wind.
The paired butterflies are already yellow with August

Over the grass in the West garden;
25 They hurt me. I grow older.
If you are coming down through the narrows of the river Kiang,
Please let me know beforehand,
And I will come out to meet you
                As far as Cho-fu-Sa.

The Eagle That Is Forgotten

VACHEL LINDSAY

(John P. Altgeld. Born December 30, 1847; died March 12, 1902)

Sleep softly . . . eagle forgotten . . . under the stone.
Time has its way with you there, and the clay has its own.

"We have buried him now," thought your foes, and in secret rejoiced.
They made a brave show of their mourning, their hatred unvoiced.
5 They had snarled at you, barked at you, foamed at you day after day.
Now you were ended. They praised you, . . . and laid you away.

The others that mourned you in silence and terror and truth,
The widow bereft of her crust, and the boy without youth,
The mocked and the scorned and the wounded, the lame and the poor
10 That should have remembered forever, . . . remember no more.

Where are those lovers of yours, on what name do they call
The lost, that in armies wept over your funeral pall?
They call on the names of a hundred high-valiant ones,

A hundred white eagles have risen the sons of your sons,
15 The zeal in their wings is a zeal that your dreaming began
The valor that wore out your soul in the service of man.

Sleep softly, . . . eagle forgotten, . . . under the stone,
Time has its way with you there and the clay has its own.
Sleep on, O brave-hearted, O wise man, that kindled the flame—
20 To live in mankind is far more than to live in a name,
To live in mankind, far, far more . . . than to live in a name.

Monologue

Reviewing the Selections

Answer each of the following questions. You may look back at the poems if necessary.

Recalling Facts

1. The river merchant's wife asks her husband to
   - ☐ a. buy her a present.
   - ☐ b. let her know when he is coming home.
   - ☐ c. clear away the moss at the gate.
   - ☐ d. be careful while he is away.

Understanding Main Ideas

2. One main idea in "The Eagle That Is Forgotten" is that
   - ☐ a. people sometimes deserve to be forgotten.
   - ☐ b. the eagle is an endangered species that needs to be protected.
   - ☐ c. a person's accomplishments are more important than his or her reputation.
   - ☐ d. a person who is forgotten after death has been defeated.

Placing Events in Order

3. In "The River Merchant's Wife: A Letter," the wife comes to love her husband
   - ☐ a. when they are both children.
   - ☐ b. at the time of their wedding.
   - ☐ c. about a year after their wedding.
   - ☐ d. after he leaves on a trip.

Finding Supporting Details

4. "Phyllis, who stands next to me, / had long hair before the glue machine / got it." What do those lines in the second stanza of "Factory Work" suggest?
   - ☐ a. Phyllis and the speaker are good friends.
   - ☐ b. Phyllis is a fast but careless worker.
   - ☐ c. The glue machine is not as bad as people might think.
   - ☐ d. The work in the shoe factory can be dangerous.

5. "Sleep on, O brave-hearted, O wise man, that <u>kindled</u> the flame." In this context *kindled* means
   - ☐ a. put out.
   - ☐ b. ignited.
   - ☐ c. sharpened.
   - ☐ d. shaded.

Interpreting the Selections

Answer each of the following questions. You may look back at the poems if necessary.

6. In the last stanza of "The River Merchant's Wife: A Letter," the wife's message to her husband is that she
   - ☐ a. is eager for his return home.
   - ☐ b. hopes he is having a good time.
   - ☐ c. thinks autumn is a depressing time of year.
   - ☐ d. wishes she had told him of her love before he went away.

7. From the evidence in "The Eagle That Is Forgotten," you can tell that John P. Altgeld
   - ☐ a. is more famous now than when he was alive.
   - ☐ b. angered many people.
   - ☐ c. was a saintly man whom everyone loved.
   - ☐ d. was successful in everything he did.

8. In "The Eagle That Is Forgotten," part of the author's purpose is to
   - [ ] a. honor John P. Altgeld.
   - [ ] b. write an inscription for Altgeld's tombstone.
   - [ ] c. shame the people who have forgotten Altgeld.
   - [ ] d. make fun of Altgeld's enemies.

Comparing

9. The language of "Factory Work" is different from the language in the other two poems in that it is more
   - [ ] a. ungrammatical.
   - [ ] b. like ordinary conversation.
   - [ ] c. serious.
   - [ ] d. old-fashioned.

Drawing
Conclusions

10. In "Factory Work" the speaker tells about two accidents, but then says, "It's not bad here." From that statement you might conclude that the speaker
    - [ ] a. likes the factory owners.
    - [ ] b. enjoys making shoes more than other jobs she has had.
    - [ ] c. accepts the danger as an ordinary part of the job.
    - [ ] d. is well paid for her work.

Monologue

Every poem has a speaker—a voice that talks. The speaker may be the poet, but not necessarily. The speaker may be a character that the poet has created. In some poems the speaker may even be an animal or an object. When you read a poem, you should always try to identify the speaker. Knowing who or what the speaker is helps you to understand a poem's meaning.

Many poems have only one person as the speaker. Such a poem is called a monologue. The speaker, however, may be addressing one or more people. In some poems, the speaker is talking to an absent friend or a loved one. In others, the speaker may be talking to the world in general or to a particular group of people.

In this lesson you will identify the voices and audiences in the three poems you have just read.

The Speaker in "Factory Work"

In the first line of "Factory Work," you learn quite a bit about the speaker: "All day I stand here, like this." You know that one person is talking and showing something to someone else. Since the title of the poem is "Factory Work," you can guess that "all day" refers to what the person does all day in the factory. "I stand here, like this" tells you that the person is standing in a particular way in a particular place.

In the next few lines you learn where the person stands—"over the hot-glue machine"—and how the person stands—"not too close to the wheel / that brings up the glue." Finally, you learn what the person does:

> and I take those metal shanks,
> slide the backs of them in glue
> and make them lie down
> on the shoe-bottoms, before the sole
> goes on.

In those lines you have a description of the speaker's job.

1. Look at lines 9 to 13. What does the speaker think of the work? Is the speaker a man or a woman?

In the first stanza the speaker, who remains nameless, has provided only basic information. In the second stanza the picture begins to develop. In a casual way, the speaker tells you about two accidents that occurred.

2. In your own words, describe the two accidents.

The work, you learn, is dangerous. Accidents occur in this factory. But the danger doesn't seem to bother the speaker. "It's not bad here," she says, "people leave you alone, don't ask you what you're thinking."

What the Speaker Reveals. When people talk, they often reveal more about themselves than they realize. For example, if you had just seen a basketball game and couldn't remember the final score, people might conclude that you did not care about the game. If someone tells a funny story, the kind of story reveals something about the storyteller's sense of humor. In a well-written monologue, similar revelations about the speaker's character, or personality, take place.

In stanza 2 of "Factory Work," you learn more about the speaker. She talks about two accidents and then says, "It's not bad here." You may begin to wonder if she has any idea how dangerous her job is. Yet she seems to accept the dangers in her job as part of living.

In stanza 3 the speaker reveals more about herself, and you develop an even clearer image of her. She thinks about the previous night when strange things happened in her apartment—"like someone was trying / to communicate to me." She mentions that her recently dead grandfather's soul might have "moved into the apartment." He might be responsible for the eggs falling and the lamp breaking. Those accidents might be a message from him.

3. If the speaker's grandfather were trying to send a message, what do the accidents suggest the message might be?

In the last stanza the speaker tells you that some workers are going to be laid off.

4. Who or what is "Eastland"? How does the company plan to choose which workers will be kept on the job? Is the speaker likely to keep her job? Explain your answer.

The speaker explains that she works automatically: "I almost / don't need to look at what / I'm doing." She lets her mind wander. She thinks of the October air where each morning "you begin / to see your breath rise / out of you like your own ghost / each morning you come here."

5. You learn about the dangers of the speaker's job. You also know that the speaker doesn't acknowledge the dangers. Given those facts, what do you think the poet is suggesting in the last few lines?

The Poet and the Speaker. The poet, Deborah Boe, has deliberately created a final image of the speaker's ghost, or soul, rising out of her as she goes in to work. The factory worker, however, is unaware of what the ghost (or any of the other images in the poem) mean. The speaker's lack of awareness of things is part of the character that the poet has created.

The factory worker, who speaks in the poem, and Deborah Boe, who wrote the poem, are two different people. Boe created the voice you hear in the poem. The voice that the poet creates is called the <u>persona</u>. In Latin, *persona* means mask. The speaker is not the poet but the poet's character.

6. Choose one of the poems that you read earlier in this book. Briefly describe the persona in that poem.

The Speaker's Audience

Think about the title of the second poem, "The River Merchant's Wife: A Letter." From it, you learn that the poem is a letter. In the poem you learn that the river merchant's wife is writing the letter to her husband, who is away on business. She looks back on their lives: childhood, marriage (arranged by their parents, according to Chinese custom), and love. She tells how she misses her husband and longs for his return.

In this poem, as in "Factory Work," the persona, or voice, is that of a young woman. There is an important difference, however, in the two personas. Each woman addresses a different audience. In "Factory Work," the speaker is talking directly to an audience. In "The River Merchant's Wife: A Letter," the speaker is addressing a specific person: her husband. In this poem you are an audience of one who reads another person's letter.

7. What other poem have you read in this book that has an audience of one? (It's also a love poem.)

Not much "happens" in Ezra Pound's poem. The richness of the poem lies in the images that Pound creates to describe the young woman's feelings. In the first line the girl describes the style of her hair: "still cut straight across my forehead." You can guess that this kind of haircut was a sign of childhood. The next few lines create a picture of two children playing in old China. The children have no "dislike or suspicion" of each other.

In the next stanza, "At fourteen I married My Lord you," the girl moves from childhood to womanhood. Once she is married, she starts revealing her feelings. At first, she is shy of her husband. Then her shyness turns to love.

8. *Look at the following images. What feeling is suggested by each?*

   a. *"Lowering my head, I looked at the wall."*
   b. *"I desired my dust to be mingled with yours*
      Forever and forever and forever."
   c. *"The monkeys make sorrowful noise overhead."*

In the last stanza Pound creates several beautiful images to express the young wife's loneliness. The woman's eagerness to meet her husband on his return shows how much she loves him. The last stanza contrasts strongly with her earlier shyness and scowling.

9. *What image or images in the last stanza show the passage of time?*

Apostrophe

The speaker in the third poem, "The Eagle That Is Forgotten," is also addressing a specific audience: John P. Altgeld. The speaker seems to be standing by Altgeld's grave and talking to him. As you will recall, the method of addressing a thing or an absent person as though they were present is called apostrophe.

Why does the poet use apostrophe? The audience of Vachel Lindsay's poem is a bystander who is listening to the speaker. Unlike the audience's situation in "The River Merchant's Wife: A Letter," the audience of "The Eagle" is not in the position of casually overhearing the speaker. The speaker obviously *wants* other people to listen. Although the speaker's words are addressed to Altgeld, their real purpose is to tell the world about Altgeld.

The eagle in the title of the poem is John P. Altgeld. During his lifetime, Altgeld was called the "Lone Eagle." Even if you did not know that fact, you could still get an idea of what Altgeld was like. The image of the eagle is carried throughout the poem.

10. *What does an eagle symbolize? Review what you learned about Altgeld in About the Selections. How might Altgeld's character be like that of an eagle?*

The poem opens with the speaker addressing the dead Altgeld: "Sleep softly . . . eagle forgotten . . . under the stone." In the second and third stanzas, the speaker makes the point that both Altgeld's friends and his enemies have forgotten him. In the fourth stanza the speaker asks where Altgeld's supporters are now. The answer is that they have turned into "a hundred high-valiant ones, / A hundred white eagles have risen the sons of your sons." In other words, many people are carrying on the work that Altgeld began, even though they may not remember his name.

11. Reread the poem's last two lines. What is the main point of those lines?

Questions for Thought and Discussion

The questions and activities that follow will help you explore the three poems in this chapter in more depth and at the same time develop your critical thinking skills.

1. **Identifying the Author's Purpose.** What do you think is the author's purpose (or purposes) in "Factory Work"? Support your opinion with quotations from the poem.

2. **Evaluating.** In "Factory Work" and "The River Merchant's Wife: A Letter," you hear the voices of two very different young women. After reading both poems, which woman do you feel you know better? Why?

3. **Supporting an Opinion.** "The Eagle That Is Forgotten" states that "To live in mankind is far more than to live in a name." What does that line mean? Do you agree or disagree with the speaker's opinion on that issue? Give reasons for your answer.

4. **Recognizing Figurative Language.** Find at least two examples of figurative language in "Factory Work." Identify what figure of speech each example is, such as metaphor, simile, or personification.

Writing About Literature

Several suggestions for writing projects follow. You may be asked to complete one or more of these projects. If you have any questions about how to begin a writing assignment, review Using the Writing Process, beginning on page 249.

1. **Explaining an Idea.** In this chapter you learned how the speaker in "Factory Work" indirectly revealed things about herself. Choose one of the other poems in this chapter and explain what you learn about the speaker that the speaker may not realize he or she is revealing. Use lines from the poem to support your ideas.

2. **Comparing.** Select three poems from the first six chapters in this book, and describe the persona in each. Then compare the characters of the speakers in the poems you chose.

3. **Apostrophizing.** Think of a person who is dead but whom you admire. The person might be someone you knew, such as a family member or friend. Or it might be a person about whom you have read or heard. Write a paragraph or two praising the person by speaking directly to him or her. Reread "The Eagle That Is Forgotten" and "O Captain! My Captain!" to understand how the poets add emphasis to their speakers' words.

4. **Writing a Letter.** Write a letter to someone you feel strongly about. In your letter describe an experience you both shared. Try to express how you felt about the experience. You may write the letter in prose or in poetry form.

Selections	***Grass***
	CARL SANDBURG

A Deserted Barn

LARRY WOIWODE

Break, Break, Break

ALFRED, LORD TENNYSON

Lesson *Personification and Speakers*

❖

About the Selections

If you visit the battlefield at Gettysburg, Pennsylvania, today, you will see a peaceful rural scene. If you walk along the ridges or hills and look out across the grassy valleys, you will find it hard to believe that thousands of people died there. Yet Gettysburg was the scene of a terrible Civil War battle. The fighting raged for three days, from July 1 to July 3, 1863.

If you had visited Gettysburg on July 4, 1863, the day after the battle ended, you would have seen more than forty thousand Union and Confederate soldiers killed or wounded. Many of the dead and wounded lay where they fell on the field. Large numbers of wounded died before they could be taken to hospitals.

As the days passed, the scene gradually changed. The wounded were carried to hospitals. The dead were either taken to their hometowns for burial or were buried in the huge battlefield cemetery. Four months after the battle, President Abraham Lincoln delivered his famous Gettysburg Address to dedicate part of the battleground as a war cemetery.

The other signs of war disappeared, too. Cannons were removed, ammunition was gathered up, and fences were repaired. Eventually, the grass grew over the broken ground. After a few years, only the monuments built by the survivors to honor their dead remained to remind visitors of the horror that had taken place at Gettysburg.

Carl Sandburg's poem "Grass" was published in 1918, when World War I was raging in Europe. The United States had not yet entered the war, but American newspapers carried detailed accounts of the battles of Ypres (EE-pruh) and Verdun. Reporters told of casualties that numbered in the tens of thousands. Sandburg's poem reminded readers that what grass and time had done to memories of past wars it would do to the memories of this latest war when it ended.

Carl Sandburg was born in 1878 in the Illinois prairie town of Galesburg. Because his family was poor, he had to leave school at the age of thirteen. He spent many of his teen years working at odd jobs. He later returned to Galesburg, where he worked as a fireman to earn money to pay for college. After leaving college, he earned his living as a journalist.

Sandburg published a small collection of poems in 1904, but it was not until 1916, with the publication of *Chicago Poems,* that he became well known. Sandburg's poems are written in free verse—verse without rhyme or meter. Walt Whitman, you will recall, shocked people in the mid-1800s when he wrote in free verse. Even though most poetry today is written in free verse, it was still controversial when Sandburg was a young man. Sandburg's poems were also unusual in his day because he used colloquial, or everyday, language to write about ordinary subjects. He wrote about subjects that farmers and factory workers would understand.

Sandburg won fame for both his poetry and his biographies. He produced a six-volume work on Abraham Lincoln that won many awards.

Larry Woiwode, the author of "A Deserted Barn," grew up in North Dakota and Illinois. Woiwode is a free-lance writer who has published several novels as well as books of poetry. He has taught writing in universities around the country. Most recently, he has been at the State University of New York in Binghamton. The poem that you will read was included in Woiwode's award-winning novel *Beyond the Bedroom Wall.* The book traces a family through three generations.

The last poem in this chapter, "Break, Break, Break," is by Alfred,

Lord Tennyson. The poet was born Alfred Tennyson in 1809. Later in life, when he was made a baron, he became Lord Tennyson.

Tennyson began writing poetry at an early age. He published his first collection of verse when he was sixteen. He published nothing for the next ten years. His silence was due partly to illness and partly to grief over the death of his closest friend, Arthur Hallam. Tennyson was deeply affected by Hallam's early death. Much of Tennyson's poetry reflects that great sadness.

In 1842 Tennyson broke his years of silence. From then until his death in 1892, he published a continuous stream of poetry. In 1850 Tennyson was named poet laureate, or official national poet, of Great Britain.

Like William Wordsworth and John Keats, whose poems you read in Chapter 4, Tennyson was a romantic poet. His style and scope were greatly influenced by Wordsworth's interest in people's relationship to nature. Tennyson wrote on a variety of themes, and used language of great tenderness and beauty.

Lesson Preview

The lesson that follows the three poems focuses on different kinds of speakers. Unlike the poems you read in Chapter 7, two of the poems in this chapter have nonhuman voices. The questions that follow will help you identify the voices in the poems. As you read, think about how you would answer these questions.

1 Who—or what—is speaking in each poem? How do you know? What can you tell about each speaker?

2 Who is being addressed in each poem? How do you know?

3 What is the reader's relationship to the speaker in each poem? Is the reader the person being addressed? An eavesdropper? Something else?

4 In "Grass" and "A Deserted Barn," what do you think the poet gains by creating an unusual speaker?

Note: The poems in this chapter do not have difficult vocabulary.

Grass

CARL SANDBURG

Pile the bodies high at Austerlitz and Waterloo.[1]
Shovel them under and let me work—
      I am the grass; I cover all.

And pile them high at Gettysburg
5 And pile them high at Ypres and Verdun.
Shovel them under and let me work.
Two years, ten years, and passengers ask the conductor:
      What place is this?
      Where are we now?

10   I am the grass.
      Let me work.

---

1. **Austerlitz and Waterloo:** sites of great battles fought by the armies of
Napoleon Bonaparte against the forces of other European nations.

A Deserted Barn

LARRY WOIWODE

I am a deserted barn—
      my cattle robbed from me,
  My horses gone,
Light leaking in my sides, sun piercing my tin roof
5   Where it's torn.
  I am a deserted barn.

Dung's still in my gutter.
It shrinks each year as side planks shrink,
Letting in more of the elements,
10   and flies.

Worried by termites, dung beetles,
  Maggots, and rats,
  Visited by pigeons and hawks,
No longer able to say what shall enter,
15   or what shall not,
  I am a deserted barn.

  I stand in Michigan,
A gray shape at the edge of a cedar swamp.
  Starlings come to my peak,
20 Dirty, and perch there;
       swallows light on bent
  Lightning rods whose blue
  Globes have gone to

A tenant's son and his .22.
25 My door is torn.
It sags from rusted rails it once rolled upon,
  Waiting for a wind to lift it loose;
Then a bigger wind will take out
  My back wall.

30 But winter is what I fear,
       when swallows and hawks
Abandon me, when insects and rodents retreat,
  When starlings, like the last of bad thoughts, go off,
  And nothing is left to fill me

35 Except reflections —

reflections, at noon,
From the cold cloak of snow, and
Reflections, at night, from the reflected light of the moon.

Break, Break, Break

ALFRED, LORD TENNYSON

Break, break, break,
   On thy cold gray stones, O Sea!
And I would that my tongue could utter
   The thoughts that arise in me.

5 O well for the fisherman's boy,
   That he shouts with his sister at play!
O well for the sailor lad,
   That he sings in his boat on the bay!

And the stately ships go on
10   To their haven under the hill;
But O for the touch of a vanished hand,
   And the sound of a voice that is still!

Break, break, break,
   At the foot of thy crags, O Sea!
15 But the tender grace of a day that is dead
   Will never come back to me.

Reviewing the Selections

Answer each of the following questions. You may look back at the poems if necessary.

Recalling Facts

1. The deserted barn stands
   - ☐ a. near a rocky shore.
   - ☐ b. in an old battlefield.
   - ☐ c. in the middle of a village.
   - ☐ d. at the edge of a cedar swamp.

Understanding Main Ideas

2. A main idea of "Grass" is that
   - ☐ a. battlefields should be made into parks.
   - ☐ b. people soon forget the horrors of war.
   - ☐ c. grass grows faster than other plants.
   - ☐ d. people should not forget where Gettysburg is located.

Placing Events in Order

3. In "Grass" the passengers ask the conductor where they are when they
   - ☐ a. see the piles of bodies.
   - ☐ b. pass the gravediggers at work.
   - ☐ c. see the grass-covered fields.
   - ☐ d. hear the sounds of battle.

Finding Supporting Details

4. In "Break, Break, Break" the fisherman's boy and the sailor lad show that
   - ☐ a. other people's lives go on normally even though the speaker is suffering.
   - ☐ b. people can earn a good living at sea.
   - ☐ c. people going to sea enjoy life more than those living on land.
   - ☐ d. the speaker wants people to pay more attention to him.

Personification and Speakers

5. "And the stately ships go on / To their <u>haven</u> under the hill." In this context *haven* means

☐ a. heaven.

☐ b. fleet.

☐ c. safe harbor.

☐ d. open sea.

Interpreting the Selections

Answer each of the following questions. You may look back at the poems if necessary.

6. In "Break, Break, Break" what can you infer from the following lines? "But O for the touch of a vanished hand, / And the sound of a voice that is still!"

☐ a. Someone important to the speaker has died.

☐ b. The speaker has been drowned.

☐ c. The speaker is homesick.

☐ d. The speaker's friends have abandoned him.

7. The speaker in "A Deserted Barn" is

☐ a. the tenant's son.

☐ b. a starling.

☐ c. an insect living in the barn.

☐ d. the barn itself.

8. In writing "A Deserted Barn," Larry Woiwode
probably wanted to
□ a. warn that dilapidated buildings
are dangerous.
□ b. describe the feelings suggested by
a deserted barn.
□ c. explain the harshness of Midwestern
winters.
□ d. start a movement to preserve old barns.

Comparing

9. The speakers in "Grass" and "A Deserted
Barn" are
□ a. unhappy with their lives.
□ b. things that cannot really talk.
□ c. proud of their accomplishments.
□ d. dead.

*Drawing
Conclusions*

10. In "Break, Break, Break" the speaker is
□ a. angry.
□ b. carefree.
□ c. grieving.
□ d. worried.

Personification and Speakers

In Chapter 7 you learned that each poem has its own voice, or speaker. You heard the voices of a woman factory worker, a young wife writing to her husband, and a speaker addressing a dead politician. In each poem, the speaker was a person talking or writing to another person.

Two of the poems in this chapter offer a different kind of speaker. In "Grass" and "A Deserted Barn," the voices are not those of human beings. In the third poem, "Break, Break, Break," the speaker is a person, but he is not addressing another person. He is speaking to the sea.

In this lesson you will identify the different kinds of speakers that poets use. You will also analyze how these unusual speakers affect the images in the poems.

Personification in "Grass"

When you begin reading Carl Sandburg's poem, you do not know who is speaking. Yet the speaker is addressing someone directly. Look at the first line: "Pile the bodies high at Austerlitz and Waterloo." Clearly, some disaster has caused the death of many people.

Of course, Sandburg expects you to know what happened at

Austerlitz and Waterloo. Those two villages became famous in the early 1800s because of the terrible battles that were fought near them during the Napoleonic wars. In 1805 almost twenty thousand French, Russian, and Austrian soldiers lost their lives at the battle of Austerlitz. Ten years later, at Waterloo, more than sixty thousand French, British, and Prussian soldiers died on the battlefield. The "bodies" referred to in the poem are the thousands of soldiers killed in battle.

The second line, "Shovel them under and let me work—," does not tell you who the speaker is. Then, abruptly, the speaker is revealed: "I am the grass; I cover all." The speaker is not a person but a plant. The grass announces that it will grow over the dead, covering them all.

In the second stanza the grass continues to speak. It names Gettysburg, in Pennsylvania, the site of a great Civil War battle. It names Ypres and Verdun, two bloody battle sites of World War I. Each of those battles left tens of thousands dead. "Shovel them under and let me work," the grass says again.

1. How does the grass seem to view those battles?

2. To whom do you think the grass is speaking?

Time passes—"Two years, ten years"—and people look out the windows of passing trains at those sites of violence. The people ask the conductor, "What place is this?"

3. Why are people unable to recognize the great battle sites? If the conductor tells them they are at "Waterloo" or "Gettysburg," do you think the people will recognize the names? Explain your answer.

The poem concludes with the grass saying, "I am the grass / Let me work."

4. What is the work that the grass will do? What attitude does the grass seem to have toward its work?

This poem is short and straightforward. The most intriguing aspect of it is the speaker. Sandburg has used personification to create a most unusual kind of speaker. Personification, you will recall, is a figure of speech in which a writer gives human qualities to animals, ideas, or objects.

In "Grass" Sandburg has given a voice to a plant. This huge grass meadow speaks with one voice, using the pronoun "I."

By giving a voice to the grass, Sandburg is commenting on our memories of the horrors of war. To make his point, he builds the entire poem around the image of grass. He then focuses the image on a single idea—what the grass does. He lets the grass tell the story from its own point of view.

5. In this poem what do you think Sandburg is saying about people's memories of war? How does the image of grass contribute to his theme?

Giving a Voice to an Inanimate Object

In Larry Woiwode's poem, "A Deserted Barn," you again find a speaker that is not a person. Unlike the speaker in "Grass," however, the voice in this second poem is not even alive. It is an inanimate object: an old, deserted barn.

The first line of the poem tells you at once who is speaking: "I am a deserted barn—." The poem is told from the barn's point of view. Like a person who has been abandoned, the barn feels lonely and useless. It no longer serves the purpose for which it was built. The only person who goes near it is the tenant's son, who uses it for target practice. The building is slowly falling apart.

6. What are some of the problems, fears, or complaints voiced by the deserted barn?

At certain times of the year, the barn has visitors. Some visitors, such as termites, dung beetles, maggots, and rats, are unwanted. Others, the barn does not seem to mind.

7. Which visitors does the barn seem to welcome? Why do you think it is glad to see these visitors?

The barn fears the winter, when its visitors will leave. It will be left with nothing but reflections—reflections of the snow, reflections of the moonlight. There is no life, only a pale, reflected light.

In this poem Woiwode personifies the barn by giving it human thoughts and feelings. You know that a barn does not really think or speak. Why, then, does the poet personify the barn?

One answer is that the poet can emphasize his ideas by creating stronger images. Imagine that a poet saw a deserted barn and then wrote about what it looked like. The poem might have expressions such as "I noticed that" or "It reminded me of" or "It seemed to be saying."

8. Why would a poem written in that manner have less emotional impact than Woiwode's poem?

Another reason for personifying the barn is to suggest certain comparisons. The barn is like a person because it expresses human thoughts and feelings about its life.

9. What stage has the barn reached in its life? How does it feel about this situation? What might be a parallel stage in a human being's life?

As you have read, the barn dreads the winter. It is not only isolated and lonely but also deserted by all living things. Winter brings nothing but reflections. The word *reflections* has more than one meaning. One meaning is memories or reminiscences. Another meaning is images, or likenesses, that are thrown back, as reflections in a mirror.

10. Reread the last four lines of the poem. What do you think the word reflections *means in those lines? How are the barn's reflections similar to those that a person might experience at a similar stage in life?*

The Speaker and the Audience

In the third poem, "Break, Break, Break," the speaker is a person. He is standing on a rocky coast, watching the waves break over the rocks. The speaker is thinking. As his thoughts take shape, he addresses them to the sea: "Break, break, break, / On thy cold gray stones, O Sea!" The speaker seems to be crying out to the harsh, cold action of the sea.

Like Vachel Lindsay in "The Eagle That Is Forgotten" (see Chapter 7), Tennyson uses apostrophe. Apostrophe is often closely related to personification. In Lindsay's poem the speaker addresses a dead person, John P. Altgeld. In Tennyson's poem, however, the speaker is addressing the sea as though it were a listening person.

There are other differences between the two poems. In "The Eagle That Is Forgotten," the speaker seems to be making a speech over Altgeld's grave. The words are addressed to Altgeld, but they are intended to be heard by any bystanders who care to listen. In "Break, Break, Break" the speaker seems to be alone. He does not expect anyone except the sea to hear the thoughts he expresses.

What are the speaker's thoughts? Apparently, some cannot be put into words: "I would that my tongue could utter / The thoughts that arise in me." Whatever those thoughts are, they appear to be sad ones. The speaker is distracted by the joys of others because their joy only intensifies his grief.

11. What images remind the speaker that other people are happy?

The speaker's thoughts turn to the "vanished hand, / And the sound of a voice that is still!"

12. What do you think the speaker is referring to in those images?

In the final stanza the speaker again addresses the sea as it breaks over the rocks. The sea continues on its course eternally. By contrast, things do not continue unchanged in the speaker's life. Something has gone from his life that will never return.

13. What has caused a change in the speaker's life? What is the contrast between the life of the sea and that of the speaker?

14. Why do you think the poet has the speaker address the sea directly?

Questions for Thought and Discussion

The questions and activities that follow will help you explore the three poems in this chapter in more depth and at the same time develop your critical thinking skills.

1. **Evaluating.** What images or details in "A Deserted Barn" give you a clear mental picture of what the barn looks like? Which do you think are most effective? Why?

2. **Drawing a Conclusion.** Besides the sea, what is the subject of "Break, Break, Break"? What words or lines in the poem lead you to this conclusion?

3. **Taking a Stand.** Do you think having plants or inanimate objects "talk" is an effective way of writing a poem? Explain your opinion, using examples from the poems in this chapter.

4. **Comparing.** Compare the mood and theme of "Break, Break, Break" to those of "The Eagle That Is Forgotten" in Chapter 7 and those of "O Captain! My Captain!" in Chapter 6.

Writing About Literature

Several suggestions for writing projects are given below. You may be asked to complete one or more of these projects. If you have any questions about how to begin a writing assignment, review Using the Writing Process, beginning on page 249.

1. **Writing in Another Voice.** Choose an object in the room in which you are now working. Write a few paragraphs or stanzas in which the object is the speaker. In that voice, show what the object does, how it feels, and what it sees. Include details about the object that say something about your feelings.

2. **Describing a Personal Experience.** Choose one of the poems in this chapter and explain its mood. Then, in a paragraph or two, describe an experience in which you experienced a similar mood.

3. **Reporting on Research.** Find out more about one of the battles mentioned in Carl Sandburg's poem "Grass." In an oral or written report, explain the events leading up to the battle and the outcome of the battle.

Chapter 9

Selections

Lord Randal

TRADITIONAL

Two Friends

DAVID IGNATOW

Reason

JOSEPHINE MILES

Lesson

Poems with More Than One Voice

❖

About the Selections

The first poem, "Lord Randal," is based on a traditional folk song that was probably first written down in the sixteenth century. No one knows exactly when or where it originated.

The poem, however, may have originated in the following way: Many centuries ago a young man had a fatal illness. His name may have been "Randal." One moment, Randal felt fine; the next, he had terrible pains. Within a short time, he was dead.

Naturally, his family and friends were shocked and saddened. Perhaps a friend wrote a song about Randal. The song told about the young man's death. It might have described the kind of person Randal was and how his friends felt about his sudden death.

Travelers heard the song and carried it to distant places. The song was never written down because at the time few people knew how to read or write. As the years passed, everyone who had actually known Randal died, but the song survived.

The song developed a life of its own. Singers who had never known Randal began to focus more on the young man's sudden death. Details were added to make the song more interesting. Perhaps the story was confused with another story about a man whose girlfriend had poisoned him.

Over hundreds of years, the song grew to contain the facts and the conversation between Lord Randal and his mother that you are about to read. Then, about four hundred years ago, "Lord Randal" was written down. The language of this version is that of southern Scotland, but there are many versions of "Lord Randal" recorded at different times.

A song like "Lord Randal," one that tells a story and that has passed from generation to generation by word of mouth, is called a ballad. About two hundred years ago, the ballad tradition was dying out because more people were learning to read. A few enthusiasts decided to record as many ballads as they could before all were lost from memory, and many old ballads have been preserved.

The story told in a ballad is usually dramatic. The narrator uses action and conversation to build the poem to a climax, or point of highest tension. As you read the poem, notice how the poet relies on conversation to develop the tragic story.

The other two poems in this chapter were written in the United States in this century. "Two Friends" is by David Ignatow and records a conversation between two people. Ignatow was born in Brooklyn, New York, in 1914. He has lived mostly in the New York metropolitan area. He has held many jobs, including salesman, public relations writer, editor, shipyard worker, journalist, president of a bindery, and college poetry teacher.

Ignatow's poems are usually about city people. The poet looks beneath the surface of city dwellers' lives to reveal what one critic has called the "bare, frequently terrifying truth." According to that critic, "Ignatow provides us with the dreams of the city-dwellers, dreams disclosing the real nature of their lives."

Like the first two poems, "Reason," by Josephine Miles, has more than one speaker. The poem records an argument. Although the poet does not use quotation marks to set off the conversation, you can determine who is speaking.

Josephine Miles was born in Chicago in 1911 but lived most of her life in California. She taught English at the University of California for many years. Miles's poems are remarkable for her use of everyday language and fresh insights, as you will see in "Reason."

Lesson Preview

The lesson that follows the three poems focuses on how poets may use more than one voice. Each of the poems has more than one speaker. When you read the poems, pay attention to how many voices are speaking and to what each speaker is saying.

The questions that follow will help you to identify the roles that the different speakers play. As you read, think about how you would answer these questions.

1 "Lord Randal" includes quotation marks that tell you when one speaker stops and another begins. But you do not really need that punctuation because the language of the poem makes the change of speakers obvious. What other signal lets you know that the speaker has changed?

2 In "Lord Randal" what elements are repeated in each stanza? Why do you think that repetition is used in the poem?

3 In "Two Friends" what can you tell about the friendship between the two speakers?

4 How many speakers do you think there are in "Reason"? What can you tell about the character of each speaker?

Note: The poems in this chapter do not have difficult vocabulary.

Lord Randal

TRADITIONAL

"O where hae ye been, Lord Randal, my son?
O where hae ye been, my handsome young man?"
"I hae been to the wild wood; mother, make my bed soon,
For I'm weary wi' hunting, and fain wald lie down."

5 "Where gat ye your dinner, Lord Randal, my son?
Where gat ye your dinner, my handsome young man?"
"I din'd wi' my true-love; mother, make my bed soon,
For I'm weary wi' hunting, and fain wald lie down."

"What gat ye to your dinner, Lord Randal, my son?
10 What gat ye to your dinner, my handsome young man?"
"I gat eels boiled in broo;[1] mother, make my bed soon,
For I'm weary wi' hunting, and fain wald lie down."

"What became of your bloodhounds, Lord Randal, my son?
What became of your bloodhounds, my handsome young man?"
15 "O they swell'd and they died; mother, make my bed soon,
For I'm weary wi' hunting, and fain wald lie down."

"O I fear ye are poison'd, Lord Randal, my son!
O I fear ye are poison'd, my handsome young man!"
"O yes! I am poison'd; mother, make my bed soon,
20 For I'm sick at the heart, and I fain wald lie down."

---

1. **broo:** broth.

Two Friends

DAVID IGNATOW

I have something to tell you.

I'm listening.

I'm dying.

I'm sorry to hear.

5 I'm growing old.

It's terrible.

It is, I thought you should know.

Of course and I'm sorry. Keep in touch.

I will and you too.

10 And let know what's new.

Certainly, though it can't be much.

And stay well.

And you too.

And go slow.

15 And you too.

Reason

JOSEPHINE MILES

Said, Pull her up a bit will you, Mac, I want to unload there.
Said, Pull her up my rear end, first come first serve.
Said, Give her the gun, Bud, he needs a taste of his own bumper.
Then the usher came out and got into the act:

5   Said, Pull her up, pull her up a bit, we need this space, sir.
Said, For God's sake, is this still a free country or what?
You go back and take care of Gary Cooper's[1] horse
And leave me handle my own car.

Saw them unloading the lame old lady,
10 Ducked out under the wheel and gave her an elbow,
Said, All you needed to do was just explain;
Reason, Reason is my middle name.

---

1. Gary Cooper: a popular star who often played the hero in Western movies.

Reviewing the Selections

Answer each of the following questions. You may look back at the poems if necessary.

Recalling Facts

1. In "Lord Randal" what does the young man tell his mother that he ate for dinner?
   - ☐ a. eels
   - ☐ b. salmon
   - ☐ c. beef stew
   - ☐ d. venison

Understanding Main Ideas

2. A main idea of "Two Friends" is that
   - ☐ a. you can always count on your friends when you need them.
   - ☐ b. good friends should tell each other everything.
   - ☐ c. people don't always pay attention to what others are saying.
   - ☐ d. aging and death are part of life.

Placing Events in Order

3. In "Reason" one speaker tells the usher to "take care of Gary Cooper's horse"
   - ☐ a. after everyone has left.
   - ☐ b. after the old lady has gone away.
   - ☐ c. before the old lady gets out of the car.
   - ☐ d. before anyone else speaks.

Finding Supporting Details

4. When Lord Randal's mother asks about his bloodhounds, he tells her that they are dead. That information supports the idea that Lord Randal
   - ☐ a. has been visiting his girlfriend.
   - ☐ b. does not take good care of his dogs.
   - ☐ c. loves hunting.
   - ☐ d. has been poisoned.

5. "For I'm weary wi' hunting, and <u>fain</u> wald lie down." In this context *fain* means
   - ☐ a. starving.
   - ☐ b. gladly.
   - ☐ c. fainting.
   - ☐ d. slowly.

Interpreting the Selections

Answer each of the following questions. You may look back at the poems if necessary.

6. From what happens in "Reason," you can infer that the action takes place
   - ☐ a. along a highway.
   - ☐ b. near Gary Cooper's house.
   - ☐ c. in a parking lot.
   - ☐ d. in front of a movie theater.

7. In "Two Friends" the sentence "Keep in touch" is evidence that
   - ☐ a. the speakers have been good friends for many years.
   - ☐ b. all friendships end sooner or later.
   - ☐ c. one friend has not been listening to what the other has been saying.
   - ☐ d. these two people have had the same conversation many times.

*Finding the
Author's Purpose*

8. Which of the following statements best describes the main theme of "Reason"?
   - ☐ a. to protest parking regulations
   - ☐ b. to show the need for simple explanations
   - ☐ c. to describe the hard life of the elderly
   - ☐ d. to explain that people are always arguing

Comparing

9. In which poem do you hear more than two speakers?
   - ☐ a. "Lord Randal"
   - ☐ b. "Two Friends"
   - ☐ c. "Reason"
   - ☐ d. all of the above

*Drawing
Conclusions*

10. In "Two Friends" the person who says, "Certainly, though it can't be much," means that there won't be much news because he or she
    - ☐ a. leads a dull life.
    - ☐ b. hasn't long to live.
    - ☐ c. is too busy to write.
    - ☐ d. doesn't like to write letters.

Poems with More Than One Voice

All the poems you have read so far in this book have had only one speaker. In Chapters 7 and 8 you looked at different speakers in various poems. Some poets, however, use more than one voice in their poems. Poets may create two or more characters, each of whom has a "speaking role." Thus, these poems contain <u>dialogue</u>, or the actual conversation between the characters.

The dialogue in these poems may serve one or more purposes. It shows what the individual characters are like, moves the action along, and helps develop the theme, or underlying message, of the poem.

In this lesson you will look at three dialogue poems to see what purposes the dialogue achieves in each.

Dialogue and Action in a Ballad

"Lord Randal" is an example of a poem with two speakers, or two people talking. First one asks a question. Then the other answers.

1. Who are the two speakers in the poem? Which one is asking the questions?

Certain images in the poem have been withheld from you. You do not know what happened between Lord Randal and his truelove. Yet through the question-and-answer dialogue, the action and events of the poem become clear. Young Lord Randal has been hunting in the woods. He has dined with his "true-love" and has returned home feeling ill. When Lord Randal's mother expresses her fear that her son has been poisoned, he agrees. The poem implies that the poisoner is Lord Randal's truelove.

As you have read, "Lord Randal" is a ballad. Like most ballads, it probably grew out of a folk story that was passed by song from generation to generation. Ballads have common characteristics that helped people to memorize them. One characteristic is that a ballad tells a simple story.

Many ballads contain epithets. An epithet is a descriptive word or phrase that expresses a quality or characteristic of an object or a person. King Richard I of England, for example, was called "Richard the Lion-Hearted." "Lion-Hearted" is an epithet. An epithet is often used in place of the name of the person or thing. Shakespeare, for instance, calls a rooster "the trumpet of dawn." In a ballad an epithet aids in identifying a character and helps the listener keep track of who is speaking to whom.

2. What epithet is used in "Lord Randal"? Where is it used?

Most ballads are written in four-line stanzas. Many use repetition of lines or stanzas. In "Lord Randal" each stanza begins with a question. Although the questions change, their form is the same. The last two lines of each stanza answer the question.

Many ballads have a refrain—one or more lines that are repeated regularly throughout the poem. However, some variations in the refrain may occur.

3. What is the refrain in the first four stanzas? How does it change in the last stanza? Why do you think Lord Randal uses different words in the last stanza?

Identifying the Speakers

Like "Lord Randal," "Two Friends" is a dialogue poem. It consists of only two voices talking to each other. There is no objective character telling you who these people are, what they look like, where they met, or how long they have known each other. There are no dialogue tags such as "he said," "she said," or "I said." All you have is the title, "Two Friends," and the words that the two characters speak.

The poem differs from "Lord Randal," however, in that it does not use quotation marks to show when one speaker stops and the other begins. You must determine who is speaking.

4. Reread the poem. How can you tell when one speaker has ended and the other is beginning?

"Two Friends" could have been written as a skit—a very short play—instead of as a poem. In the play the two speakers might have names or initials. You could then tell quite easily who was speaking. In this poem you have to pay close attention to the words so that you can identify the speaker. The experience is rather like overhearing a conversation in which you cannot see the speakers. You can only hear the two voices.

5. Try reading the poem by identifying the speaker in line 1 as Voice A and the speaker in line 2 as Voice B. Who is dying? Who says "Keep in touch"? Who speaks the last line?

Character and Dialogue

The opening lines of "Two Friends" suggest that the poem will be a conversation about death.

> I have something to tell you.
> I'm listening.
> I'm dying.

In line 4, however, you realize there is something wrong with this conversation. "I'm sorry to hear" is one friend's response to the news that the other is dying. Generally, a person says "I'm sorry to hear" in response to a minor crisis such as hearing that a friend has a bad cold or has to have a tooth pulled. It suggests an unpleasant experience, but it is not what you say to a person who is dying. You may begin to wonder about the character of the two speakers. In line 2 the speaker has said, "I'm listening." But just how true is that statement?

In line 5 the first speaker says: "I'm growing old." Again, the second speaker's response sounds insensitive. "It's terrible" is something you might say after someone comments on the bad weather. Still, the first speaker seems to accept the response. The comment "I thought you should know" is almost apologetic. From the friend's responses, the first speaker may realize that he or she is imposing on the friend's patience and willingness to listen.

The second speaker seems to reply sympathetically: "Of course" (meaning "Of course you should tell me") "and I'm sorry." Then the second speaker adds, "Keep in touch." That phrase signals that the conversation is over. Once again, you might question the sincerity of the speaker's earlier comment, "I'm sorry." In the last four lines both speakers exchange the standard parting comments.

6. Make a list of the second speaker's comments in lines 10 to 15. Explain what those comments tell you about the person.

In the last half of the poem, it becomes clear that the first speaker has given up on the conversation. The second speaker either has forgotten the subject of their conversation—that the first speaker is dying— or has never consciously recognized that fact. By the last two lines— "And go slow. / And you too."—the two friends are exchanging meaningless phrases.

David Ignatow's poem is full of irony—the contrast between what is said and what is meant. People use verbal irony all the time in conversation. You might say to a friend, "Great, it's raining!" However, your tone of voice says that you are not at all pleased that it is raining. You are using irony—saying one thing but meaning the opposite.

7. Look at the title of Ignatow's poem. Then think about what takes place in the conversation between the two friends. What is ironic about the poem's title?

8. Find an example of irony in one or more lines of the poem. Explain the irony.

The Speakers in "Reason"

The third poem, "Reason," differs from "Lord Randal" and "Two Friends" in two ways. First, "Reason" has more than two speakers.

9. How many speakers do you hear in the poem? Identify each speaker. Which of them speaks more than once?

Second, "Reason" differs from the other two poems in that it includes what we might call "stage directions." The word *Said* that begins several lines lets you know that the speaker is changing. It's almost like giving a name tag to a speaker. Another stage direction appears at the end of stanza 1.

10. What does that stage direction tell you?

Notice, though, that the stage directions are not as complete as they would be in the script of a play. The poet relies on you to determine who is speaking and what is taking place. Notice, too, that the stage directions are delivered by one of the speakers in the poem. When giving those stage directions, the speaker addresses you directly. At other times, the speaker is talking to the various characters in the poem.

11. Which speaker delivers the stage directions?

As you have read, "Reason" involves a conflict over a parking space in front of a movie theater. Such an argument might occur on any crowded city street. Insults are exchanged. The usher from the movie theater comes out and gets involved in the argument.

In the last stanza, however, the scene shifts from the conflict to the reason behind the first driver's request to "Pull her up a bit." A "lame old lady" is unloaded from the car. Clearly, the first driver demands the space so that he can "unload" the lady in front of the theater, but he has not told the second driver why he wants the space. The second driver is embarrassed, annoyed, and gallant as he hops out to help the old woman.

In the last two lines he justifies his actions and his irritation:

Said, All you needed to do was just explain;
Reason, Reason is my middle name.

The speaker is suggesting that if people were reasonable, if they gave reasons for their requests, perhaps there would be fewer conflicts.

12. Look at the language used in the dialogue in "Reason." Would you call it formal or informal language? Does the language of the speakers sound believable? Explain your answer.

Questions for Thought and Discussion

The questions and activities that follow will help you explore the three poems in this chapter in more depth and at the same time develop your critical thinking skills.

1. **Analyzing.** What features in "Lord Randal" make it easy to memorize? Look back at the other poems you have read in this book. Which one (or ones) do you think are similar to this ballad? Why?

2. **Taking a Stand.** Would "Two Friends" work better as a poem if it included dialogue tags for the speakers such as "he said" or "she said"? Why or why not?

3. **Identifying the Author's Purpose.** What do you think the author of "Reason" is saying about people's reasonableness? Use lines from the poem to explain your ideas.

4. **Preparing an Oral Presentation.** Divide the class into small groups. Each group should choose one of the dialogue poems in this chapter and perform the poem as though it were a staged play. Before you stage the poem, discuss what tone of voice each speaker should use to deliver his or her lines. Decide, too, at what speed the characters should speak and which words or sounds to emphasize.

Writing About Literature

Several suggestions for writing projects are given below. You may be asked to complete one or more of these projects. If you have any questions about how to begin a writing assignment, review Using the Writing Process, beginning on page 249.

1. **Inventing a Ballad.** Ballads often tell tragic stories of love, jealousy, and sudden death. They also recall daring deeds or strange adventures. Invent a story that might become the subject of a ballad. Then try composing at least two stanzas of the ballad. Remember that ballads are meant to be sung. You might want to choose a familiar tune to accompany your ballad.

2. **Comparing.** In a few short paragraphs compare the similarities and differences in the ways that "Lord Randal" and "Two Friends" tell their stories.

3. **Writing a Dialogue.** Write a dialogue of twelve to fifteen lines in which two friends meet and talk on the street. Include some clues in the dialogue that help reveal the character of each speaker.

4. **Explaining an Idea.** Listen for examples of irony in the talk around you. Then write a short paper in which you explain why you think people use irony. Be sure to include examples to support your ideas.

Understanding Poetry

*I*n the first three units, you learned a number of skills to help you read and understand poetry. You have studied one skill at a time, analyzing a poem with that particular skill in mind. In Unit Four you will need to apply all the skills you have learned to interpret the meanings of the poems.

When you read a poem, you can often find a clue to the poem's subject and meaning in its title. Sometimes the title suggests that the poem has more than one meaning. As you will see in Chapter 10, many poems have more than one level of meaning.

Discovering the levels of meaning in poetry is like exploring a town or a village. When you first approach it, you notice the main roads, the larger buildings, and the other landmarks that stand out at first glance. As you begin to explore the town, you notice the smaller streets that lead to out-of-the-way places. Perhaps you notice details on the buildings or see unusual stores that add to your understanding of the town. With a poem, too, you can experience the satisfaction of following "signs" offered by the poet to explore its different meanings.

Imagination also occupies a special place in reading and understanding poetry. The poet uses his or her imagination to create a poem. At the same time, the poet expects you to let your imagination wander freely as you listen to the sounds and experience the images of the poem. As you have seen, poetry is a compact form of writing. Poets leave out many details that prose writers might include. The poet relies on your imagination to fill in the missing details.

Sometimes you may find the meaning of a poem difficult to grasp because the poet has raised more questions than he or she has answered. When you try to answer those questions, apply the skills that you have learned in the previous chapters. Analyze the poet's use of figurative language, rhythm, meter, and so on. You will find that knowing the special language of poems will increase your understanding and enjoyment of poetry.

Selections	*Stopping by Woods on a Snowy Evening*
	ROBERT FROST

Cloud, Castle, Lake

LAWRENCE RAAB

The Tide Rises, The Tide Falls

HENRY WADSWORTH LONGFELLOW

Lesson *Levels of Meaning*

❖

About the Selections

Poets and writers have often used travelers or journeys as metaphors for the passage of life. Sometimes the metaphor is easy to find; at other times, authors disguise the metaphor in subtler ways. The three poems in this lesson seem to be simple stories about travelers. However, when you study the poems, you will discover that the poets have incorporated several levels of meaning into poems that seem plain and straight-forward.

Robert Frost's "Stopping by Woods on a Snowy Evening" is one of his most famous poems. The poem's narrator, a traveler, talks about returning home on a winter evening and stopping on the way to look at the woods around him. But as you will learn, this quiet scene can also stand for something else.

Many readers feel that Robert Frost's poetry is much easier to read and understand than the work of other modern poets. Although many of his poems, like "Stopping by Woods on a Snowy Evening," are more complicated than they appear, his simple language and rural subject matter make the poems easy to read.

Frost was born in San Francisco in 1884, but his family moved to Massachusetts when he was still a child. After leaving college, Frost bought a farm in New Hampshire. The farming venture failed, however, so he moved to England in 1912. There he published his first two books of poetry. The second collection, *North of Boston,* was well received in the United States, and by the time he returned, he had established a reputation for sophisticated poetry crafted within traditional verse forms. After his return to New Hampshire, Frost continued to write until his death in 1963.

Like the Frost poem, Lawrence Raab's "Cloud, Castle, Lake" describes a lovely scene that suggests more than one meaning. The title of Raab's poem is taken from a short story by Vladimir Nabokov, a Russian writer who emigrated to the United States. Nabokov's story, which was published in 1941, tells about a traveler who sees a wonderfully peaceful scene and wants to stay in that place. His fellow travelers, however, force him to return home with them. Raab's poem has some similarities to Nabokov's story, but the mood and theme of the two works are very different.

Like Robert Frost, Lawrence Raab is a New Englander. He was born in Pittsfield, Massachusetts, in 1946. He has spent most of his adult life in academic life. He currently teaches English at Williams College and writes poetry whenever he has the opportunity.

As the title of the third poem suggests, "The Tide Rises, The Tide Falls" is set along a shore. In the poem the traveler leaves footprints in the sand, but the tide's movements erase the footprints, and the traveler—like his footprints—is seen no more.

Henry Wadsworth Longfellow, who wrote "The Tide Rises, The Tide Falls," is the author of some of the best-known American poems. The most ambitious were long narrative poems, such as "Evangeline" and "Hiawatha."

Longfellow was born in Portland, Maine, in 1807. He studied European languages and literature in college and on trips to Europe. A scholar in modern languages, Longfellow taught French and Spanish at Bowdoin College and Harvard University. Longfellow was an extremely popular poet during his lifetime, as well as a well-respected teacher and translator.

Longfellow's poetry has melody, clear expression, and a kind of gentleness. Those qualities have helped to make his poems as popular today as they were during his lifetime.

Lesson Preview

The lesson that follows the three poems focuses on the different levels of meaning that can be found in poetry. When you look at a poem closely, you often discover that it has more than one meaning. Each of the poems in this chapter concerns a traveler. In each, however, the image of the traveler and his journey is a metaphor for life.

The questions that follow will help you find the different levels of meaning in the poems. As you read, think about how you would answer these questions.

1 What happens in "Stopping by Woods on a Snowy Evening"? What does the speaker decide to do in the end?

2 As you read the last stanza of "Stopping by Woods on a Snowy Evening," think about what other meanings the lines might have.

3 What happens in the second poem? How is the situation of the traveler in "Cloud, Castle, Lake" similar to that of the traveler in "Stopping by Woods on a Snowy Evening"? How is it different?

4 How do the last two stanzas of "Cloud, Castle, Lake" help explain the rest of the poem?

5 What happens in "The Tide Rises, The Tide Falls"? How does this poem resemble the other two poems? How does it differ from them?

Vocabulary

Here are some difficult words that appear in the poems that follow. Study the words and their definitions, as well as the sentences that show how the words are used. This will help you get the most from your reading.

parapets a wall or elevation of earth or stone to protect soldiers. *As we walked along the parapets of the old castle, we had an excellent view of the countryside around us.*

eluded escaped from, by quickness or cunning. *Although the thief eluded the police for several hours, he was finally caught and taken to the station.*

resign give up. *The professor is hoping to resign from academic life and retire to the country.*

tranquil calm; peaceful. *The pond is often tranquil and still in the early morning.*

ravine a small, narrow, steep-sided valley. *Over many years, the river had hollowed its bed into a deep ravine.*

efface erase; rub out. *Because the beach was part of a wildlife preserve, the rangers tried to efface all signs of human damage to the area.*

Stopping by Woods
on a Snowy Evening

ROBERT FROST

Whose woods these are I think I know.
His house is in the village though;
He will not see me stopping here
To watch his woods fill up with snow.

5 My little horse must think it queer
To stop without a farmhouse near
Between the woods and frozen lake
The darkest evening of the year.

He gives his harness bells a shake
10 To ask if there is some mistake.
The only other sound's the sweep
Of easy wind and downy flake.

The woods are lovely, dark and deep,
But I have promises to keep,
15 And miles to go before I sleep,
And miles to go before I sleep.

Cloud, Castle, Lake

Lawrence Raab

After a story by Vladimir Nabokov

Quietly, concealing himself in his own shadow,
he followed the shore and came to a kind of inn.
Beyond it lay the blue lake, the black
parapets of a castle, and a single cloud
5   set also in the center of the water.

Amazed, he knew at once the promise
of that happiness which had always eluded him.
A small room for travelers was available—
red floors, the simple bed and bureau,
10   a mirror full of yellow flowers from the wallpaper,

and a window framing the lake
and its cloud and castle.
There was so little of his life
to change, it would not be difficult
15   (he decided in a moment) to resign,

and send for the few possessions he wanted—
books and a blue suit, a photograph
of the woman he had loved quite hopelessly
for the past seven years.
20   "I shall take it for the rest of my life,"

he said, although even then he could hear
from the far side of the lake
the cries of his fellow travelers.
They would be marching toward him,
25 because no one could be left behind.

And he would be made to join them
and sing the songs of the other travelers.
This tranquil scene, like such words as
"for the rest of my life," would be cast aside
30 and trampled underfoot, in their pleasure.

Before that afternoon he had seen glimpses
and he knew, as you must know,
how many landscapes summon us
as we pass in a train, for example,
35 with no hope of stopping or of turning back.

The blue dampness of a ravine.
A memory of love, disguised as a meadow.
Presented, and quickly taken back.
So unfairly, so predictably. Which was,
40 upon his return, all that he could tell me.

The Tide Rises, The Tide Falls

HENRY WADSWORTH LONGFELLOW

The tide rises, the tide falls,
The twilight darkens, the curlew[1] calls;
Along the sea-sands damp and brown
The traveler hastens toward the town,
5   And the tide rises, the tide falls.

Darkness settles on roofs and walls,
But the sea, the sea in the darkness calls;
The little waves, with their soft, white hands,
Efface the footprints in the sands,
10   And the tide rises, the tide falls.

The morning breaks; the steeds in their stalls
Stamp and neigh, as the hostler[2] calls;
The day returns, but nevermore
Returns the traveler to the shore,
15   And the tide rises, the tide falls.

---

1. curlew: a large, wading shorebird.   **2. hostler:** a person who takes care of horses at a stable.

Reviewing the Selections

Answer each of the following questions. You may look back at the poems if necessary.

Recalling Facts

1. In "Cloud, Castle, Lake" the traveler wants to
   - ☐ a. spend the rest of his life in a small room in an inn.
   - ☐ b. watch a woods filling up with snow.
   - ☐ c. live in a castle, where he will never have to work.
   - ☐ d. walk along a beach.

Understanding Main Ideas

2. A main idea of "Stopping by Woods on a Snowy Evening" is that
   - ☐ a. the snow makes the trees look different in winter.
   - ☐ b. a lonely road in the woods is a good place to stop and think about life.
   - ☐ c. there is no stopping in one place in life, no matter how lovely.
   - ☐ d. a person should not make too many promises, because promises can tie you down.

Placing Events in Order

3. In "Cloud, Castle, Lake" the traveler sends for "the few possessions he wanted"
   - ☐ a. after looking out the window of a train.
   - ☐ b. as soon as he sees the room in the inn.
   - ☐ c. only in his hopes and dreams.
   - ☐ d. after he hears the voices of the other travelers.

4. In "Stopping by Woods on a Snowy Evening," the sound of the harness bells
   - ☐ a. contrasts with the complete silence of the woods.
   - ☐ b. signals that the speaker has decided to move on.
   - ☐ c. suggests that the horse senses an animal in the woods.
   - ☐ d. shows that another traveler is approaching.

5. "The morning breaks; the <u>steeds</u> in their stalls." In this context *steeds* means the
   - ☐ a. sheep.
   - ☐ b. horses.
   - ☐ c. guests at the inn.
   - ☐ d. roosters.

Interpreting the Selections

Answer each of the following questions. You may look back at the poems if necessary.

6. In the first line of "Cloud, Castle, Lake," the man is "concealing himself in his own shadow." From this phrase you can infer that the man is
   - ☐ a. a magician.
   - ☐ b. hiding from his friends.
   - ☐ c. a criminal on the run.
   - ☐ d. walking outside on a bright, sunny day.

7. "The day returns, but nevermore / Returns the traveler to the shore." Those lines from "The Tide Rises, The Tide Falls" suggest that the traveler has
   - ☐ a. returned home.
   - ☐ b. died.
   - ☐ c. left the area.
   - ☐ d. any of the above.

8. One purpose of the author in "Stopping by Woods on a Snowy Evening" is to
   - ☐ a. suggest how the woods look and sound during a snowfall.
   - ☐ b. show that travelers must pass through different landscapes.
   - ☐ c. explain why the woods are dangerous.
   - ☐ d. compare winter and summer.

9. "The Tide Rises, The Tide Falls" differs from the other two poems in that the
   - ☐ a. traveler is walking instead of riding.
   - ☐ b. traveler probably does not continue on his journey.
   - ☐ c. poet never identifies the traveler.
   - ☐ d. speaker and the traveler are different people.

10. In the last poem the refrain "And the tide rises, the tide falls" suggests that the
    □ a. traveler in the poem has drowned.
    □ b. world goes on regardless of what happens to any one person.
    □ c. traveler loves to watch the tide but is afraid of it.
    □ d. tides are getting higher because of the full moon.

Levels of Meaning

As you learned in earlier chapters, you can read a poem several times and find more meaning in it each time. By looking at the images, language, and sounds in a poem, you can usually discover additional meanings. Most poems can be read in more than one way. That is, a poem often has different levels of meaning. The first time you read a poem, you gather its surface meaning. By reading it several times, you can begin to interpret other meanings.

The deeper levels of meaning in poetry do not reveal themselves immediately, and interpretations of a poem can vary. As a result, different people find different meanings in a poem. Usually, you cannot prove that a particular interpretation of a poem's meaning is the "correct" one. However, a good interpretation is based on the poet's words, and not on the reader's idea of what the poet *ought* to have meant. In this lesson you will look at the levels of meaning in three poems.

"Stopping by Woods on a Snowy Evening"

"Stopping by Woods on a Snowy Evening" is probably one of the best-known poems written by an American in this century. The reasons for its popularity are not hard to find. First, its language is simple. Anyone can read the poem without difficulty. Second, the situation described in the poem is also simple and easy to understand.

Third, the poem "sounds" right. Frost seems to have found the exact words to capture the quiet beauty of a snowfall. Finally, when you reread the poem, you find that it is about much more than falling snow. It has another level of meaning that becomes clear if you read carefully.

The Surface Meaning. The first time you read a poem, you find the most obvious, or surface, meaning. Look again at Robert Frost's poem. Its first level of meaning is simple. A traveler has stopped to watch the snow as it falls in the woods near the road. Except for his horse, he is alone. There are no farms or other buildings to be seen. It is so quiet that the traveler can actually hear the snow fall. The speaker finds the woods beautiful. Then he reminds himself that he must move on because he is still a long way from his destination.

1. Why do you think the traveler might be passing through the woods described in Frost's poem?

2. What is the setting—the time and place—of the poem? Use evidence from the poem and from Frost's background to suggest an answer.

The language of the poem is simple and clear. Except for the first line, the language is that of everyday conversation.

In the first line the poet reverses the normal word order. Ordinarily, a person would say, "I think I know whose woods these are." In the poem the line reads, "Whose woods these are I think I know." The reversal of word order contributes to the rhyme pattern of *know, though,* and *snow.* It also emphasizes the word *woods.* In this way, the poet draws your attention to the importance of the woods in the poem.

3. Describe the rhyme scheme of the poem. How does it connect the stanzas? How does it change in the last stanza?

A Second Level of Meaning. By carefully reading the poem, you can discover another level of meaning. Look for that level of meaning in the things that are stressed in the poem—the things that stand out as important. One clue has already been given. The woods, of course, are prominent in Frost's poem. They may have another level of meaning. Notice also the repetition of the last line.

The deeper meaning of the poem comes into focus in the last stanza. Read it once more. It begins, "The woods are lovely, dark and deep." Say that line out loud several times and think about what it means and how it sounds. Remember that the traveler is thinking those words as he looks into the woods. The woods are tempting him to leave the road entirely—to stop his journey.

The road the traveler is journeying on can be seen as a metaphor for life. Along that road, he is tempted to stop in a peaceful place. The peaceful place can be interpreted as death. To someone weary of life, death may seem to offer a "lovely, dark and deep" beauty.

But the traveler shakes off the temptation. Like the horse who has impatiently given a shake to his harness bells, the speaker shrugs off his weary thought: "But I have promises to keep."

That line is the reason why the traveler rejects the temptation. Although the traveler is alone on the road at that moment, he is not alone in the world. He has responsibilities to the people who care about him and who depend on him.

Notice that the last two lines are repeated: "And miles to go before I sleep. / And miles to go before I sleep." Those lines suggest that there is still much living to be done. It is not yet time to sleep—or to die.

Much of the enjoyment of reading poetry lies in uncovering and understanding the various levels of meaning in poems. If you think you have found a deeper level of meaning in a poem, read the poem again, looking for details that support your interpretation.

4. Think about the following details in Frost's poem and explain how you might interpret the meaning of each: (a) the fact that the traveler is alone, (b) the "frozen lake," (c) the line that reads, "The darkest evening of the year."

"Cloud, Castle, Lake"

Lawrence Raab's poem, too, can be understood on more than one level. Like Frost's poem, "Cloud, Castle, Lake" is about a traveler who is tempted to drop out of a journey.

The Surface Meaning. The traveler leaves the main road and comes to a place that seems perfectly suited to him. At an inn he finds a small room that is perfect for him. He wants to settle there for the rest of his life. But he instantly realizes that he will not be allowed to remain. He has been traveling with other people who will catch up with him and force him to continue the journey.

At the end of the poem the speaker reflects that many people often see a landscape that summons them to stop. But they are unable to answer that summons.

5. Look at the last two stanzas of the poem. How do they differ from the rest of the poem?

Other Levels of Meaning. On the surface level this poem and "Stopping by Woods on a Snowy Evening" appear to have similar themes. As you look into the deeper meanings of each poem, however, you see that they are different.

The major difference lies in what tempts each traveler to leave the road—to quit the journey. In Frost's poem the traveler is tempted to give up life for the rest offered by death. In "Cloud, Castle, Lake" the traveler is tempted by a different way of life—a way that appeals to him more than his present way of living.

The difference between the temptations suggests another difference. Think about the roads that the two men have been traveling. In Frost's poem the road is a metaphor for life itself. In "Cloud, Castle, Lake" the road represents just one way of life. The traveler's choice in this poem is not between life and death but between one way of living and another.

6. What do you think the images of the cloud, castle, and lake represent?

The reasons each traveler decides to continue are also very different. In "Stopping by Woods on a Snowy Evening," the traveler realizes he must live up to his responsibilities. In "Cloud, Castle, Lake" the traveler feels pressured by other travelers to return to the main road. The poem does not explain why the traveler feels pressured by his fellow travelers.

The last two stanzas of "Cloud, Castle, Lake" compare the impossibility of staying in that new, tempting place to the impossibility of stopping and exploring all the lovely places people glimpse as they pass on a speeding train. In life, the poet is saying, people have to choose to keep traveling in some direction. They can't explore in depth everything that interests them.

7. Read the poem again. Look at the following lines in the context of the whole poem. What deeper meaning do you think these lines might have?

> *This tranquil scene, like such words as*
> *"for the rest of my life," would be cast aside*
> *and trampled underfoot, in their pleasure.*

"The Tide Rises, The Tide Falls"

The third poem is also about a traveler. Like the other two selections, it has a fairly simple surface meaning.

8. In your own words summarize what happens in Longfellow's poem.

As you read the poem and wrote the summary, you probably asked yourself certain questions. Why doesn't the traveler return? Who is the traveler? Finding the deeper level of meaning of the poem depends on how those questions are answered. No doubt, you can think of many reasons why a person might walk on a beach one day and never return.

As with other poems, you can find deeper levels of meaning by looking at the ideas and images that the poem seems to stress. Notice, for example, that the title of the poem, "The Tide Rises, The Tide Falls," is repeated as a refrain. Clearly, the movement of the tide is important. The regular, rhythmic rise and fall of the tide suggests eternity. Within eternity, you find other images—the traveler, twilight, the call of the curlew, the town, the darkness of night, and the return of day.

On the surface level the traveler is one person; on a deeper level, however, the traveler stands for all people, moving through life. In poetry the images of night and day are often used as metaphors for death and life. In this poem twilight suggests the approach of darkness—the nearness of death. The call of the curlew, too, can be viewed as a signal that a life is drawing to a close. The traveler hurries toward the town, which seems to represent the warmth, life, and companionship of other people. "Darkness settles on roofs and walls" of the town, perhaps swallowing the traveler in death.

In the morning life begins again with the sounds of "the steeds in their stalls" and the hostler's calls. Yet even though life returns to the world, the traveler will not be seen on that shore—he or she has passed on into eternity.

9. Think about the traveler's footprints. Are the footprints a metaphor? What do you think is the significance of the waves wiping away the footprints?

10. What do you think the poem is saying about the importance of a person's life? Do you agree with its message? Explain.

Questions for Thought and Discussion

The questions and activities that follow will help you explore the three poems in this chapter in more depth and at the same time develop your critical thinking skills.

1. **Analyzing.** In this chapter you looked at one way of interpreting the woods in Robert Frost's poem. Divide the class into small groups. Each group should discuss what else the woods might represent. Then compare the ideas of your group with those of the other groups.

2. **Comparing.** Compare the speakers in "Stopping by Woods on a Snowy Evening" and "Cloud, Castle, Lake." How are they different?

3. **Evaluating.** Look at lines 24 to 27 in "Cloud, Castle, Lake." The poem suggests that people cannot choose to stop and change the course of their lives. Do you agree with that idea? Why or why not? Why do you think the traveler chose to rejoin the others? Do you think it was a good decision? Why or why not?

4. **Recognizing Personification.** Find an example of personification in "The Tide Rises, The Tide Falls." What effect does it have on the poem?

Writing About Literature

Several suggestions for writing projects are given below. You may be asked to complete one or more of these projects. If you have any questions about how to begin a writing assignment, review Using the Writing Process, beginning on page 249.

1. **Explaining an Idea.** Using any poem in this chapter, select one detail that seems to have more than one level of meaning. Write a paragraph or two explaining the various meanings of that detail.

2. **Describing Levels of Meaning.** Choose a poem you read in an earlier chapter. Write a paper summarizing the surface meaning of the poem and identifying the deeper meanings you find in it. Be sure to use specific words, images, phrases, or lines from the poem to support your ideas about its meaning.

3. **Describing a Scene.** Describe a landscape or a scene that has caused you to stop or pause in your daily routine. You can use prose or poetry, but your description should show why the scene made you stop and reflect.

Chapter 11

Selections   *The Great Bird of Love over the Kingdom*
PAUL ZIMMER

The Listeners
WALTER DE LA MARE

Lesson   *Fantasy, Mystery, and Imagination*

❖

About the Selections

People often invent imaginative stories about fantastic creatures and give those creatures magical powers. In "The Great Bird of Love over the Kingdom," Paul Zimmer has done just that. The great bird is called The Zimmer. Its name suggests close ties with the poet himself.

Paul Zimmer was born in Ohio in 1934. As a young man, he worked in bookstores in San Francisco. Later, he became an editor for a university publisher. In his leisure time Zimmer wrote the poetry that has earned him recognition. "Making poems is the best and most exhilarating thing I do," Zimmer has said.

In interviews Zimmer has described how he developed the different characters in his poetry. "Because of early scholastic difficulties," he said, "I was more or less forced to regard myself as a failure as a young person. Consequently, when I began writing poetry, I was not able to make poems about myself, not thinking myself important enough to write about."

Instead of writing about himself, Zimmer created a series of characters and gave each of them a voice. He created a kind of mythical world where creatures named Wanda, Imbellis, and Cecil lived.

Later, however, Zimmer gained enough confidence to begin a series of autobiographical poems. Those poems told of the joys and frustrations of his childhood and teenage years.

In "The Great Bird of Love over the Kingdom," the autobiographical and the mythical come together. The poem is autobiographical because it tells about the poet's own experiences. It talks about his dreams—or daydreams. At the same time, the poem is about a beast—the kind of beast that occurs only in mythology.

The author of the second poem, "The Listeners," is Walter de la Mare. He was born in England in 1873. After completing school, he took a job as a bookkeeper in the London office of a major oil company.

Although de la Mare kept his job, he thought of himself as a poet rather than an office worker. He wore clothes that marked him as a poet. In the early 1900s, a velvet coat and long hair were the symbols of poets. The oil company decided to let their bookkeeper-poet write a company newspaper. The experiment was a failure, and de la Mare soon returned to bookkeeping. However, he devoted his evenings and weekends to writing poetry and fiction.

By 1908, when de la Mare was thirty-five, he was earning enough from his writing to support himself and his family. He gave up his office job and moved to the country. For nearly fifty years, he lived in the country, producing more than fifty books of fiction, essays, and poetry.

De la Mare's life in the country was far from dull. He had a vivid imagination. De la Mare has been called a "master of the shadowed borderline between the real and the unreal." He took ordinary objects and events such as a candle stub or a man knocking on the door of an empty house and used them to embark on fascinating, even frightening, adventures. In "The Listeners," you will see what happens as the poet follows a lonely traveler to an empty house.

Lesson Preview

The lesson that follows "The Great Bird of Love over the Kingdom" and "The Listeners" focuses on the poet's imagination in creating fantasy and mystery. When writing poems, poets use their imaginations to communicate attitudes, feelings, and ideas. When you read poems, you must also put your imagination to work.

The questions that follow will help you find the elements of fantasy and mystery in the two poems. As you read, think about how you would answer these questions.

1 How does the poet's imagination show itself in "The Great Bird of Love over the Kingdom"?

2 How does Zimmer's poem stimulate your imagination?

3 What mysteries does the poet leave unsolved in "The Listeners"? How do these mysteries spark your imagination?

Vocabulary

Here are some difficult words that appear in the poems that follow. Study the words and their definitions, as well as the sentences that show how the words are used. This will help you get the most from your reading.

luminous giving off light; glowing in the dark. *The luminous moon cast its reflection on the dark water of the pond.*

undefiled clean; pure. *This lake is one of the few bodies of water that is still undefiled by acid rain.*

cherished treated with love. *My grandmother has always cherished the beautiful quilts her mother made.*

thronging crowding together in large numbers. *While the spectators were thronging the stage door, the actor slipped out another exit.*

hearkening listening. *Hearkening to the old man's words of warning, the hikers sought safety from the approaching storm.*

cropping cutting off the tops, as of grass. *Father was upset to discover the goat cropping the blossoms on his prize rosebushes.*

The Great Bird of Love over the Kingdom

PAUL ZIMMER

I want to become a great night bird
Called The Zimmer, grow intricate gears
And tendons, brace my wings on updrafts,
Roll them down with a motion
5 That lifts me slowly into the stars
To fly above the troubles of the kingdom.
When I soar the moon will shine past
My shoulder and slide through
The streams like a luminous fish.
10 I want my cry to be huge and melancholy,
The undefiled movement of my wings
To fold and unfold on rising gloom.

People will see my silhouette from
Their windows and be comforted,
15 Knowing that, though oppressed,
They are cherished and watched over,
Can turn to kiss their children,
Tuck them into their beds and say:
　　Sleep tight.
20 　　No harm tonight,
　　In starry skies
　　The Zimmer flies.

The Listeners

WALTER DE LA MARE

"Is there anybody there?" said the Traveler,
 Knocking on the moonlit door;
And his horse in the silence champ'd the grasses
 Of the forest's ferny floor:
5 And a bird flew up out of the turret,
 Above the Traveler's head:
And he smote upon the door again a second time;
 "Is there anybody there?" he said.
But no one descended to the Traveler;
10 No head from the leaf-fringed sill
Lean'd over and look'd into his gray eyes,
 Where he stood perplex'd and still.
But only a host of phantom listeners
 That dwelt in the lone house then
15 Stood listening in the quiet of the moonlight
 To that voice from the world of men:
Stood thronging the faint moonbeams on the dark stair,
 That goes down to the empty hall,
Hearkening in an air stirr'd and shaken
20 By the lonely Traveler's call.
And he felt in his heart their strangeness,
 Their stillness answering his cry,
While his horse moved, cropping the dark turf,
 'Neath the starr'd and leafy sky;
25 For he suddenly smote on the door, even
 Louder, and lifted his head:—
"Tell them I came, and no one answer'd,
 That I kept my word," he said.

Never the least stir made the listeners,
30   Though every word he spake
Fell echoing through the shadowiness of the still house
        From the one man left awake:
Ay, they heard his foot upon the stirrup,
        And the sound of iron on stone,
35 And how the silence surged softly backward,
        When the plunging hoofs were gone.

Reviewing the Selections

Answer each of the following questions. You may look back at the poems if necessary.

Recalling Facts

1. In "The Great Bird of Love over the Kingdom," The Zimmer is
   - ☐ a. an evil spirit.
   - ☐ b. the ghost of the poet.
   - ☐ c. a huge night bird.
   - ☐ d. a luminous fish.

Understanding Main Ideas

2. A main idea of "The Great Bird of Love over the Kingdom" is that
   - ☐ a. the great bird of love takes away people's fears.
   - ☐ b. The Zimmer will defeat the forces of evil.
   - ☐ c. all people are afraid at night.
   - ☐ d. children like to believe in fantasies.

Placing Events in Order

3. In "The Listeners" the listeners are quiet
   - ☐ a. until the traveler knocks a second time.
   - ☐ b. until the traveler calls out that he has kept his word.
   - ☐ c. until the bird flies up from the turret.
   - ☐ d. throughout the entire poem.

Finding Supporting Details

4. In "The Great Bird of Love over the Kingdom," the people are comforted because
   - ☐ a. The Zimmer has escaped.
   - ☐ b. their children are asleep.
   - ☐ c. they know they are loved.
   - ☐ d. their troubles have been ended.

Fantasy, Mystery, and Imagination

5. "And he <u>smote</u> upon the door again a second time." In this context *smote* means
   ☐ a. opened.
   ☐ b. struck hard.
   ☐ c. shut.
   ☐ d. looked.

Interpreting the Selections

Answer each of the following questions. You may look back at the poems if necessary.

6. In "The Great Bird of Love over the Kingdom," you can infer that "the troubles of the kingdom" are caused by
   ☐ a. economic troubles such as high prices and unemployment.
   ☐ b. disease and hunger.
   ☐ c. the burdens of life.
   ☐ d. a civil war.

7. In "The Listeners" what can you tell about the traveler?
   ☐ a. He is a knight in armor.
   ☐ b. He once lived in the house he is visiting.
   ☐ c. He is an old man.
   ☐ d. He is a man with a horse.

Finding the
Author's Purpose

8. In "The Listeners" the author's purpose appears to be to
   - ☐ a. make the reader think about death.
   - ☐ b. tell about an experience he once had.
   - ☐ c. create a mysterious scene.
   - ☐ d. frighten the reader.

Comparing

9. Unlike the speaker in "The Great Bird of Love over the Kingdom," the speaker in "The Listeners" is
   - ☐ a. the poet himself.
   - ☐ b. an object and not a person.
   - ☐ c. a person who knows and explains exactly what is happening.
   - ☐ d. an observer outside the action of the poem.

Drawing
Conclusions

10. The speaker in "The Great Bird of Love over the Kingdom" wants to
    - ☐ a. conquer the world.
    - ☐ b. comfort and protect people.
    - ☐ c. blot out the moon.
    - ☐ d. fly into outer space.

Fantasy, Mystery, and Imagination

As you have read, many poets write about everyday subjects. Some poets talk about ordinary events such as working in a factory or watching football. Yet they make those everyday events seem special by using strong images. The language, imagery, and structure in their works create strong feelings.

Some poems that you have read are narratives—they tell stories. In "The Cremation of Sam McGee" and "The Raven," the speakers relate strange tales. Other poems deal with subjects such as love, the death of a famous person, the beauties of nature, and the stages of human life. In each poem, the poet has used his or her imagination to create a powerful work with strong images, feelings, and ideas.

In this lesson you will read the works of two poets who go beyond the subject matter of everyday life to explore other dimensions. The poems of Paul Zimmer and Walter de la Mare can be compared to the works of science fiction and fantasy writers. Authors of science fiction and fantasy go beyond reality to deal with magic, the supernatural, or the strange possibilities of science. In this "other dimension," writers expect you to be prepared to accept the unusual, the strange, or the unexplained.

Fantasy and Reality in
"The Great Bird of Love over the Kingdom"

Paul Zimmer mixes fantasy and reality in his poem. He sets the poem in an everyday world where people struggle with the burdens of life. Yet high above that ordinary world soars an extraordinary magical beast called The Zimmer. It is "a great night bird" whose purpose is to protect and comfort the people living in the world below.

The speaker imagines himself as The Zimmer. He will move his wings to rise "slowly into the stars / To fly above the troubles of the kingdom." Many centuries ago, people believed that the stars formed a kind of envelope around the earth. A powerful magical bird like The Zimmer could certainly soar into those nearby stars.

1. Look carefully at the poem. What other words or actions suggest a fairy tale, or fantasy, world?

The poet tells you that he is creating a fantasy. In the first line and a half, he says: "I want to become a great night bird / Called The Zimmer . . ." That statement can be compared to the famous opening words of many fairy tales: "Once upon a time." Both openings let you know that you are about to hear a "made-up" tale. Both the storyteller and the listener know the difference between the real world and the fantasy to come.

Zimmer's fantasy world contains other reminders of the real world. The Zimmer sees that there are "troubles" in the kingdom. The speaker does not, however, tell you what those troubles are. Instead, you are left to speculate, or guess what they might be.

2. What do you think the "troubles" are that threaten the kingdom? How does The Zimmer's appearance ease those troubles?

Tone. You can identify a poet's tone by carefully reading the poem. As you have learned, tone refers to the poet's attitude toward his or her subject, audience, or self. For example, the tone of a poem can be playful, serious, sarcastic, or sympathetic. A poet might express more than one attitude, and the tone can even change in the course of a poem. You can discover the tone of a poem by recognizing the poet's attitude toward his or her character and by looking carefully at the words the poet has chosen.

In the first stanza of "The Great Bird of Love over the Kingdom," the speaker describes The Zimmer, telling you what it looks and sounds like.

3. Reread the first stanza. Give one or two adjectives to describe the feelings that the poet expresses toward his subject. How does the author's tone influence your feelings toward The Zimmer?

In the second stanza you learn why the speaker wants to become The Zimmer. People who look up and see the bird's silhouette will be comforted. They will feel protected. Children can sleep unafraid because "In starry skies / The Zimmer flies."

Why The Zimmer's appearance comforts people is not made clear. But the title of the poem suggests an answer. The Zimmer is a "Great Bird of Love." It will bring the power of love to comfort the people.

4. Think about the tone of the second stanza. Is it the same or different from the tone of the first stanza? Explain your answer.

Levels of Meaning. As you learned in Chapter 10, poems can have more than one level of meaning. In "The Great Bird of Love over the Kingdom," you are introduced into a fantasy world in which The Zimmer plays an important role. What lies beneath the surface of the poem? What underlying ideas and issues exist in the poet's fantasy?

As you answer those questions, remember that there is no single right answer. Any response that can be supported by the language of the poem is a good interpretation.

The speaker says that he would like to become The Zimmer. There must be reasons why he wants to be that particular kind of bird. The reasons have to do with how the speaker sees himself and how he would like other people to see him.

5. What does the speaker want for himself? What does he want for other people? How does he see himself in relation to other people?

6. Think about the title of the poem. What word appears in the title that does not appear in the poem itself? How does it help answer question 5?

The Mystery in "The Listeners"

Walter de la Mare's poem introduces you to a strange and eerie world. Like Paul Zimmer's poem, it has elements of fantasy. Through his imagination, the poet has created a mystery. He also challenges you to use your own imagination to solve the mystery.

In the opening lines a traveler knocks on a "moonlit door" and calls out, " 'Is there anybody there?' " When there is no reply, he tries again. He is "perplex'd" by the lack of response, and calls out again. This time he shouts a longer message:

> "Tell them I came, and no one answer'd,
>   That I kept my word," he said.

The man then mounts his horse and leaves. Those few incidents make up the entire action of the poem. Yet, as the title suggests, there is more meaning than this summary reveals.

The poem is full of mysteries. Who is the traveler? Why has he come? He apparently expected to find someone at the house. Why is no one there to answer his knock? Even though no one answers him, someone or something is listening. Those "phantom listeners" are at the heart of the mystery.

7. Who or what do you think are the phantoms? Where have the people gone? Suggest as many answers to those questions as you can imagine.

The poet does not tell you who the listeners are. By not doing so, he encourages you to come up with possible answers. The more you use your imagination to solve the mystery, the richer the poem becomes. In the end, however, the mystery remains.

Details and Images. The poet heightens the sense of mystery through the use of details. Early in the poem, you learn that the traveler has arrived at night, because he knocks on a "moonlit door." Inside and outside the house, all is silent.

8. What noises break the silence? How do those sounds add to the sense of mystery?

The traveler is aware of the "phantom listeners":

> And he felt in his heart their strangeness,
> Their stillness answering his cry,

His awareness of someone or something listening makes him knock even louder. The poet uses the word *smote* to emphasize the force of the traveler's knocking. The traveler also cries out a message to the phantom listeners, just in case they are real.

Perhaps you have experienced a similar feeling. Have you ever been in an empty house or room when suddenly you felt sure that someone was there? Have you spoken aloud to the imagined presence? Think about the reasons why you spoke out loud.

By using various details, the poet suggests that the listeners are real. He tells us that they stand listening to the voice of the traveler. Even though they remain silent and still, they hear the traveler mount his horse and ride off. Despite those details, you are still left wondering whether or not the listeners are real. If they are real, why don't they answer?

Levels of Meaning. The many questions raised by this poem help you to explore beyond the surface meaning. But the poem is not a solvable puzzle. You won't find the answers hidden somewhere in its lines. Instead, you have to find answers in your own imagination.

In thinking about the deeper meaning of "The Listeners," think about the words of the traveler: " 'Tell them I came . . . / That I kept my word.' " The traveler has kept a promise, but no one seems to care. To what situations in life might this apply? Perhaps the poem is saying something about promises being kept too late to do any good. Maybe the promise has lost its purpose because conditions have changed.

9. Develop a possible interpretation of "The Listeners." Then explain why you think it is a good interpretation of the poem.

Questions for Thought and Discussion

The questions and activities that follow will help you explore the two poems in this chapter in more depth and at the same time develop your critical thinking skills.

1. **Interpreting.** Why do you think Paul Zimmer invents The Zimmer as a bird? In your imagination, what other kind of creature could it have been? Explain your choice.

2. **Analyzing.** Sound and silence are important in "The Listeners." In the poem find examples of how the poet's use of language creates a contrast between those two elements.

3. **Identifying the Author's Purpose.** Walter de la Mare probably had more than one purpose in writing "The Listeners." Identify one purpose he might have had in writing the poem. Give reasons for your choice.

4. **Evaluating.** Which poem in this chapter do you think requires the greater use of your imagination? Explain your answers.

5. **Comparing.** Other poems, such as "Lord Randal" or "The Tide Rises, The Tide Falls," leave you with unsolved questions. Compare the mysteries in one of those poems to the mysteries in "The Listeners."

Writing About Literature

Several suggestions for writing projects follow. You may be asked to complete one or more of these projects. If you have any questions about how to begin a writing assignment, review Using the Writing Process, beginning on page 249.

1. **Describing a Fantasy.** Imagine that you could transform yourself into a magical creature. Write several paragraphs describing the creature you would choose to be. Include a physical description and an explanation of the creature's magical powers. Then tell how you would use your powers.

2. **Explaining an Opinion.** Do you like poems or stories that spell out everything that happens, or do you prefer poems or stories that leave you with unanswered questions? Explain your preference.

3. **Writing About a Personal Experience.** What is the most mysterious experience you have ever had? In a short paper, describe what happened and how you felt about the experience. Try to include details that show the sense of mystery you felt.

Chapter 12

Selections   *Kidnap Poem*

NIKKI GIOVANNI

Constantly Risking Absurdity

LAWRENCE FERLINGHETTI

Sonnet 18: Shall I Compare Thee to a Summer's Day

WILLIAM SHAKESPEARE

Lesson   *Poets on Poetry*

❖

About the Selections

No matter what kind of work people do, they have opinions about the importance of their work. A lawyer has his or her own view about the law. A farmer has his or her own ideas about growing crops. Poets also have their own opinions about the nature and purpose of poetry. In the poems in this chapter, you will see how three poets view their art.

The first poem is by Nikki Giovanni. She was born in Knoxville, Tennessee, in 1943. She has always been a fighter. In her autobiography, *Gemini: An Extended Autobiographical Statement on My First Twenty-Five Years of Being a Black Poet*, Giovanni tells how at the age of four she attacked and drove off some children who were picking on her sister. Her sister was several years older.

During the 1960s, Giovanni became deeply involved in the black revolutionary movement. Her first collection of poetry, published in 1968, supported her strong political views. Giovanni's subsequent work has continued to express her anger at racism and sexism.

Despite the often violent nature of her poems, Nikki Giovanni is a cheerful person with a playful sense of humor. She had a happy childhood in a warm and loving family. Her childhood memories have influenced her view of life and, of course, her poetry. As you will see, these two sides of the poet—the warm, loving person and the fighter—come together in "Kidnap Poem."

The second poem, "Constantly Risking Absurdity," is by another American poet, Lawrence Ferlinghetti. He was born in 1919 in a New York suburb. Ferlinghetti served in World War II. After the war, he finished college and then studied at the University of Paris. After graduating, he moved to San Francisco where he opened City Lights Bookshop, a bookstore that became famous in the 1950s.

In the 1950s a group of writers and their friends came together in San Francisco to share ideas. They called themselves the "beat generation." They soon became known as "beatniks," in mimicry of the Soviet satellite *Sputnik,* which was launched in the late 1950s. The beatniks often met at City Lights Bookshop, where they read their poetry.

The beatniks might be called "the fighting dropouts." They rejected the values held by middle-class Americans in the 1950s. They called life in the United States a "rat race" because they felt that most people were driven by a desire for money and material goods. The beatniks preferred to drop out of the rat race. They adopted what they considered a more casual and less materialistic way of life.

At the same time, the most outspoken leaders of the beat generation did more than just drop out. They saw themselves as intellectuals and reformers. They set out to tell anyone who would listen what was wrong with life in the United States. They expressed their views in novels, poetry, and autobiographies. Much of their writing was published by Lawrence Ferlinghetti.

Ferlinghetti wrote poetry, and eventually he was recognized as one of the best poets of the beat generation. Since the 1950s, many ideas of the beat generation have influenced the mainstream of American life. Ferlinghetti has continued to write and speak on many political and social issues. In the poem in this chapter, however, he tells how it feels to be a poet.

The last poem in the book is a sonnet by William Shakespeare. In

Chapter 2 you read Shakespeare's poem "The Seven Ages of Man."

Shakespeare is probably best known for his plays. Among them are *Romeo and Juliet, Julius Caesar,* and *Macbeth.* In 1609, however, toward the end of his career, a book of 154 of his sonnets was published. All the sonnets are love poems. The book is dedicated to a person identified only by initials. No one really knows for whom they were written. There are a few tantalizing clues. Some sonnets refer to a "dark lady," but no one has ever been able to discover her identity.

Most people agree that the sonnets are among Shakespeare's finest poetry. The poem you will read is Sonnet 18. Shakespeare did not give his sonnets titles. However, they are often referred to by the words of their first lines. Sonnet 18 is also known as "Shall I Compare Thee to a Summer's Day."

Lesson Preview

The lesson that follows the three poems focuses on the views of several poets on poetry. Their views are expressed in poems that they wrote *about* writing poetry. Each poet looks at poetry from a different angle. The questions that follow will help you discover what each poet is saying about poetry. As you read, think about how you would answer these questions.

1 In "Kidnap Poem," who is being kidnapped? By whom? Why? In what sort of prison is the kidnapped person to be kept?

2 To whom is the poet compared in "Constantly Risking Absurdity"? How does Ferlinghetti make the point that writing a poem can be risky?

3 The poem "Constantly Risking Absurdity" is an extended metaphor. How do the details in the poem reinforce the metaphor?

4 Shakespeare's sonnet "Shall I Compare Thee to a Summer's Day" begins with a question. How does the poem answer the question?

5 The sonnet concludes by suggesting that poets have a special power. What is that power?

Poets on Poetry

Vocabulary

Here are some difficult words that appear in the poems that follow. Study the words and their definitions, as well as the sentences that show how the words are used. This will help you get the most from your reading.

complement to complete a whole. *The curator chose this painting to complement the other paintings on display in the gallery.*

taut tight, not slack. *Please pull the tape measure taut so that we get an accurate measurement.*

temperate moderate; self-restrained. *Although our temperate climate does not usually produce heavy snowstorms, we have had several feet of snow this year.*

Kidnap Poem

NIKKI GIOVANNI

ever been kidnapped
by a poet
if i were a poet
i'd kidnap you
5   put you in my phrases and meter
you to jones beach
or maybe coney island[1]
or maybe just to my house
lyric[2] you in lilacs
10 dash you in the rain
blend into the beach
to complement my see
play the lyre[3] for you
ode[4] you with my love song
15 anything to win you
wrap you in the red Black green[5]
show you off to mama
yeah if i were a poet i'd kid
nap you

---

1. **jones beach/coney island:** Jones Beach and Coney Island are two large public beaches on the Atlantic coast to which residents of New York City and other nearby communities flock in the summer. **2. lyric:** a poem that expresses the poet's emotions and thoughts. **3. lyre:** a stringed instrument used in ancient times by poets when they sang their verses. **4. ode:** originally, a poem written to be sung. Today, an ode is typically a poem addressed to a person or thing. It has an elaborate style and expresses lofty feelings. **5. red, Black, green:** the colors of the flag of the black power movement.

Poets on Poetry

Constantly Risking Absurdity

LAWRENCE FERLINGHETTI

Constantly risking absurdity

          and death

     whenever he performs

         above the heads

5   of his audience

   the poet like an acrobat

      climbs on rime

        to a high wire of his own making

and balancing on eyebeams

10   above a sea of faces

     paces his way

       to the other side of day

   performing entrechats[1]

      and sleight-of-foot tricks

15 and other high theatrics

      and all without mistaking

   any thing

      for what it may not be

---

1. entrechats: in ballet, leaps straight upward during which the dancer crosses his or her legs a number of times.

For he's the super realist

20   who must perforce[2] perceive

taut truth

                before the taking of each stance or step

in his supposed advance

                toward that still higher perch

25   where Beauty stands and waits

                with gravity

                    to start her death-defying leap

And he

        a little charleychaplin[3] man

30   who may or may not catch

her fair eternal form

            spreadeagled in the empty air

of existence

---

2. perforce: by necessity.   **3. charleychaplin:** Charley Chaplin was one of the best-known comic actors of the silent movies.

Sonnet 18
Shall I Compare Thee to a Summer's Day

WILLIAM SHAKESPEARE

Shall I compare thee to a summer's day?
   Thou art more lovely and more temperate:
Rough winds do shake the darling buds of May,
   And summer's lease hath all too short a date:
5 Sometime too hot the eye of heaven shines,
   And often is his gold complexion dimmed;
And every fair from fair sometime declines,
   By chance, or nature's changing course untrimmed;[1]
But thy eternal summer shall not fade,
10   Nor lose possession of that fair thou owest,[2]
Nor shall Death brag thou wanderest in his shade,
   When in eternal lines to time thou growest;
      So long as men can breathe, or eyes can see,
      So long lives this, and this gives life to thee.

1. untrimmed: deprived of elegance; stripped of ornament.   **2. owest:** have, possess.

Reviewing the Selections

Answer each of the following questions. You may look back at the poems if necessary.

Recalling Facts

1. In "Constantly Risking Absurdity" a poet is compared to a
   - ☐ a. lion tamer.
   - ☐ b. tightrope walker.
   - ☐ c. stockbroker.
   - ☐ d. clown.

Understanding Main Ideas

2. Which of the following statements summarizes a main idea of "Shall I Compare Thee to a Summer's Day"?
   - ☐ a. Fewer people die in summer than in winter.
   - ☐ b. Despite the warmth and beauty of summer, it is a harsh season that kills many people.
   - ☐ c. Poets think that summer days go on forever.
   - ☐ d. Through the poem, the person to whom the poet is speaking will live forever.

Placing Events in Order

3. In "Kidnap Poem" which of the following things does the speaker plan to do first?
   - ☐ a. take the kidnapped person out in the rain
   - ☐ b. wrap the kidnapped person "in the red Black green"
   - ☐ c. "meter" the kidnapped person to Jones Beach
   - ☐ d. show the kidnapped person off to her mother

4. In "Shall I Compare Thee to a Summer's Day,"
what does the poet mean by saying, "And
often is his gold complexion dimmed"?
☐ a. A person's face becomes paler as he
or she grows older.
☐ b. The summer sun is sometimes covered
by clouds.
☐ c. The speaker knows that he or she is
dying.
☐ d. People often get tanned in summer.

5. "before the taking of each stance or step /
in his supposed advance / toward that still
higher perch / where Beauty stands and
waits." In this context *perch* means a
☐ a. resting place.
☐ b. ladder.
☐ c. yellow fish.
☐ d. multistory building.

Interpreting the Selections

Answer each of the following questions. You may look back at the poems
if necessary.

6. The speaker in "Constantly Risking
Absurdity" believes that writing poetry
☐ a. helps a poet become a better
entertainer.
☐ b. forces a poet to appreciate other people.
☐ c. is the only worthwhile activity in life.
☐ d. is as dangerous as performing high-wire
acrobatics.

7. In "Kidnap Poem" the kidnapped person
is going to be
   - ☐ a. held for ransom.
   - ☐ b. tortured.
   - ☐ c. put into a poem.
   - ☐ d. drowned in the ocean.

8. In "Shall I Compare Thee to a Summer's Day,"
Shakespeare probably repeats "so long" in the
last two lines to
   - ☐ a. remind readers that death is
     everywhere.
   - ☐ b. reinforce the image of summer.
   - ☐ c. emphasize the idea of eternity.
   - ☐ d. compare death and eternity.

9. In both "Kidnap Poem" and "Shall I Compare
Thee to a Summer's Day," the speakers
   - ☐ a. are addressing someone who has died.
   - ☐ b. talk as if a person can be turned into
     a poem.
   - ☐ c. claim that a poem will make a person
     immortal.
   - ☐ d. want to take someone home.

10. After reading "Constantly Risking Absurdity,"
you can conclude that the poet
   - ☐ a. has worked in a circus.
   - ☐ b. is close to death.
   - ☐ c. thinks writing poetry is very risky.
   - ☐ d. finds it easy to write about beauty.

Poets on Poetry

You have read more than two dozen poems in this book. In each, the poet has taken a different approach to writing verse. The works vary. The poets have chosen a range of subjects, from love and death to the beauty of daffodils and the strange events of an Arctic night. They have used different kinds of speakers to address a variety of audiences. The line lengths, meter, and rhyme are different. The poets have used similes, metaphors, and other kinds of figurative language, and they have created a range of images. Some images are startling or frightening. Others are simple and direct.

Just as the works of poets vary, so, too, do their views of poetry and the art of writing poetry. From time to time, a poet stops to think about what it is like to write poetry. What does the poet do? What does a poet capture in a poem? The three poems in this chapter examine the poet's view of his or her work.

The Poet and the Speaker in "Kidnap Poem"

In her poem Nikki Giovanni's subject is thought of as a serious and violent crime—kidnapping—but she turns it into a lighthearted and kindly act. The contrast between a real kidnapping and the kidnapping in this poem is important. Kidnappers usually threaten to harm the victim if their ransom demands are not met. In Giovanni's poem, however, there is no talk of ransom or threats. Instead, the speaker describes kidnapping as an imaginary act in which you sense a kind of gaiety and dedication, but no violence.

The poem contains an extended metaphor in which the poet compares the capture of a person in the lines of a poem to a kidnapping. In this case, the kidnapper is a kindly soul who treats the kidnapped victim with playful kindness and care.

1. What actions show that the speaker plans to treat the kidnapped person in a kindly way? What feelings does the speaker seem to have toward the kidnapped person?

The poem tells you what the speaker would do if she were a poet. Yet Nikki Giovanni is a poet. Why would a poet choose to use the persona, or voice, of someone who is not a poet? One possible explanation is that by using a different voice the poet can explain what poets try to do.

In her poem Giovanni suggests that poets do, in fact, capture people by putting them into poetry. Think of the poems you have read about people, such as Walt Whitman's "O Captain! My Captain!" and Gwendolyn Brooks's "Martin Luther King Jr." In those poems the poets put their subjects into their own phrases and meter. As Giovanni implies, the captured person—the subject of the poem—can do nothing about his or her situation. The person is at the mercy of the poet. The poet may do "anything to win you" and may even "show you off to mama."

2. List at least four ways in which the speaker in "Kidnap Poem" would try to "win" the kidnapped person. Which way or ways are most closely connected with the writing of poetry?

3. The poem has a lighthearted tone. How does the poet establish that tone?

Poets on Poetry

Simile and Metaphor in "Constantly Risking Absurdity"

Nikki Giovanni suggests how a poet can capture a person in a poem. In the second poem Lawrence Ferlinghetti talks of the risks that a poet takes in writing a poem.

The title of the poem, "Constantly Risking Absurdity," shows where the risk lies. In trying to capture beauty, the poet is in danger of sounding silly or ridiculous.

Creating an Extended Metaphor. In the second stanza of the poem, the speaker uses a simile to compare the poet to an acrobat. Ferlinghetti develops that comparison throughout the poem, creating an extended metaphor. All the acts, the risks, of a poet are compared to the acts of an aerial acrobat. The poet-acrobat performs tricks high above the audience. He must risk failure to be a success. One false step on the tightrope can send him crashing to the ground.

4. What are some skills that an acrobat must have? How are those skills similar to the skills a poet needs?

In the poem the poet-acrobat climbs "toward that still higher perch / where Beauty stands and waits . . ." Then he becomes a trapeze artist who "may or may not" catch Beauty as she sails through the air. The risk is tremendous. If he fails, Beauty will be lost.

The poet's role is described as "a little charleychaplin man." In his early movies Charlie Chaplin played a sad but lovable character called "the Little Tramp." The Little Tramp wore clothes that were too big and walked in a peculiar way. He was a timid soul with a bashful smile. The Little Tramp always tried to be helpful, but he either failed or did not get credit if he succeeded.

5. In lines 29 to 33, the poet tries to catch Beauty's "fair eternal form / spreadeagled in the empty air." Why might a poet feel like Charlie Chaplin's Little Tramp when trying to catch beauty?

Metaphor and Levels of Meaning. The use of metaphor always indicates that the poet is writing on more than one level. A metaphor, after all, is a symbol for something else. In this poem, the acrobat is a symbol for the poet. All the actions in the poem are metaphors that are symbolic of the poet's struggles. Think about the metaphor in the opening lines in which the poet-acrobat "performs / above the heads / of his audience."

6. What is the surface meaning of that image? What is the deeper meaning?

7. Choose another action in the poem and explain its surface meaning as well as its symbolic meaning.

Levels of Meaning and the Poet's Play on Words. Ferlinghetti introduces other levels of meaning when he makes puns—humorous plays on words that sound alike but have different meanings. Look, for example, at line 9 where the poet-acrobat is "balancing on eyebeams." An I-beam is a steel girder, shaped like the capital letter I, which is used in building skyscrapers. When a tall building is under construction, workers walk along the I-beams many stories above the ground. They are like acrobats on a circus tightrope. However, Ferlinghetti uses the word *eyebeams,* not *I-beams,* and he adds "above a sea of faces."

8. What does the word eyebeams *suggest about the poet-acrobat?*

9. Ferlinghetti introduces at least two other puns with the phrases "taut truth" (line 21) and "waits / with gravity" (lines 25 and 26). Say each phrase out loud a few times. What are the different meanings of the words taut, waits, *and* gravity?

Shakespeare on Poetry

"Shall I Compare Thee to a Summer's Day" is a sonnet. As you learned in Chapter 4, a sonnet is a poem written in fourteen lines. Shakespeare's sonnet is a love poem. At the same time, it is a poem that discusses its own power and the power of all poetry.

The poem begins with a question. In line 1 the speaker addresses the question to a particular person—"Shall I compare thee to a summer's day?" In other words, shall I praise you by saying that you are like a day in summer? In line 2 the speaker rejects the comparison as not good enough.

10. Summarize why the speaker decides that the comparison does not work.

In lines 3 through 8, the speaker details why the comparison doesn't work. Summer is not always "temperate"; "Rough winds do shake the darling buds of May." In Shakespeare's time, the English calendar was slightly different from our modern one. May was then a summer, not a spring, month. The speaker adds that summer doesn't last long: "And summer's lease hath all too short a date." Sometimes the sunshine is too hot. At other times, the sun is covered by clouds with its "gold complexion dimmed." What's more, even a beautiful summer day eventually ends: "every fair from fair sometime declines."

In line 9 the focus of the poem shifts from summer days to the person whom the speaker is addressing. The person's "eternal summer," or everlasting youth, will never fade as a summer day does. Nor will the person's beauty disappear. Even death will not be able to claim the person.

11. What reason does the speaker give as to why the person will live forever?

12. Sonnet 18 begins as a love poem. At the end, it is still a love poem, but it also has become a poem about poetry. At what point in the poem does the second subject appear? How can you tell?

In "Constantly Risking Absurdity" the poet is an acrobat, performing various tricks and trying to catch Beauty as she flies through the air. "Kidnap Poem" portrays the poet as kidnapper—having the power to capture a person within a poem. In his sonnet Shakespeare makes the greatest claim of all for poetry. He says that the person he is praising will be remembered for as long as "men can breathe, or eyes can see." Poetry can grant immortality to a person, at least as long as people can still read.

13. Which of these poets' views of poetry do you find most appealing? Explain your answer.

Questions for Thought and Discussion

The questions and activities that follow will help you explore the three poems in this chapter in more depth and at the same time develop your critical thinking skills.

1. **Analyzing Images.** In "Kidnap Poem" Nikki Giovanni uses a number of vivid images, or word pictures. Identify three images. Explain which of the five senses (sight, sound, taste, touch, smell) are affected by each image.

2. **Explaining Personification.** Find an example of personification in "Constantly Risking Absurdity." Why do you think the poet used that figure of speech? Why do you think Shakespeare personifies death in "Shall I Compare Thee to a Summer's Day"?

3. **Identifying the Author's Purpose.** "Shall I Compare Thee to a Summer's Day" is both a love poem and a poem about poetry. Which of these do you think is Shakespeare's main focus in the poem? Or are they equally important? Explain your view.

4. **Taking a Stand.** The poets who wrote the poems in this chapter obviously believe that what poetry accomplishes and what poets do are very important. What do you think is the role of poets? Give reasons for your answer.

5. **Comparing.** Divide the class into small groups. Each group should choose a different poem from other chapters in this book. Within your group, decide how you think the author of the poem you chose sees poetry. Use evidence from the poem to support your group's view. Each group can then share its ideas with the rest of the class.

Writing About Literature

Several suggestions for writing projects follow. You may be asked to complete one or more of these projects. If you have any questions about how to begin a writing assignment, review Using the Writing Process, beginning on page 249.

1. **Writing a Letter.** Suppose that you are the kidnapped person in "Kidnap Poem." In an effort to escape, you write a letter that will be smuggled to the outside world. In the letter describe your life in the poem and suggest how you might be rescued.

2. **Writing a Review.** Imagine that you are a critic for a local newspaper. Your assignment is to review the circus. Write a review in which you describe and evaluate the performance of the acrobat in "Constantly Risking Absurdity." Include metaphors and puns in your review.

3. **Comparing.** Review the discussion of sonnets in Chapter 4. Reread the other sonnets you studied earlier in this book: John Keats's "On the Grasshopper and Cricket" and Merrill Moore's "The Noise That Time Makes." Compare and contrast those two sonnets with Sonnet 18, "Shall I Compare Thee to a Summer's Day."

Using the Writing Process

The lesson that follows is designed to help you with the writing assignments you will meet in this book. It explains the major steps in the writing process. Read the lesson carefully so that you understand the writing process thoroughly. On pages 259–260, following the lesson, is a checklist. Whenever you are asked to complete a writing assignment, you can just refer to the checklist as a reminder of the things you should consider as you're working on the assignment. The lesson can then serve as a reference—an information source. Turn to it whenever you feel that it would be helpful to review part or all of the process.

When presented with a writing assignment, many people's instant response is panic. What will I write about? Do I have anything to say? To ease the panic, remind yourself that writing is something that *no one* simply sits down and does with the words flowing freely and perfectly from first sentence to last. Rather, writing is a *process;* that is, it involves a number of steps. The writing process is not a straightforward, mechanical one, such as that involved in solving a mathematical problem. These pages give you a plan that you can follow to sensibly work through the complex task of presenting your ideas on paper.

Keep in mind that writing is not simply the act of filling a piece of paper with words. It is a sophisticated act of communication. The purpose of writing is to put *ideas* across to other people. Since ideas come from your mind, not your pen, the writing process begins with the work that takes place in your mind: the creation and organization of ideas. The process then proceeds to the expression of ideas—the actual setting down of words on paper. The final stage is the polishing of both the ideas and the words that express them.

As they work, writers engage in a variety of activities—thinking, planning, organizing, writing, revising, rethinking. For clarity, we label the various stages in the process prewriting, writing, and revising. However, the stages are not so straightforward and separate. One blends into the next, and sometimes a writer returns to a previous activity, moving back and forth through the process. When you write, your goal should be to produce a clear and lively work that expresses interesting ideas. The writing process can help you in that effort.

Stage 1: Prewriting

Define Your Task

The first stage in the writing process is prewriting. At this stage, your goal is to choose a topic, to figure out what you are going to say about it, and to decide what style and tone you are going to use. Making these decisions is essential if you are going to write something interesting and to express your ideas clearly and vividly. At this stage you jot down thoughts and ideas—the material that you will eventually organize and write about in detail. During the prewriting stage, you should search for answers to the following questions:

What Will I Write About? This question must be answered before you do anything else. You need to choose a topic. Then you need to *focus* the topic. A focused topic directs your thinking as you write. This is important whether you are writing a brief description, a short story, an essay, or a research paper. Deciding just what issues you want to address, what kind of character you want to develop, or what theme and events you want a story to revolve around will focus your thinking and help you create a bright, strong piece of writing.

A careful decision is called for here. A good topic is neither too broad nor too narrow. The length of what you are writing and your purpose for writing often dictate how broad your focus should be. In an essay or a research paper, for instance, you need to choose a topic that's defined enough to explore in depth. You don't want to choose a topic that's so broad that you can only touch on the main ideas. If your assignment is to write a short story, you'll want to focus on perhaps one main relationship between characters, one important conflict, just a few related events. You can then write in detail to create full, interesting characters and a well-developed story. When you need to focus a topic, think about what would be practical for the given task.

What Do I Want to Say? You need to think about what information you want or need to include, and what ideas you want to communicate.

What Is My Purpose for Writing? Will you try to persuade, to inform, to explain, or to entertain your readers?

What Style Will I Use? Do you want to write formally or in a casual, conversational style? Will you use the first person, I, or the third-person, he, she, or they? Will you write seriously or use jokes and humor? If you are writing a story, will you use dialogue?

How Will I Organize My Ideas? What will you start with? In what order will you present and develop your ideas?

Who Is My Audience? Who will be reading your work? Are you writing for other students? For people who already have some background in the subject? For people who know nothing about the subject? For children or for adults? Your audience will dictate the approach you take—whether you will write in a formal or an informal tone, whether you will provide a lot of background information or very little, what kind of words you will use.

Generate and Organize Ideas

Although most of the writing assignments in this book provide fairly specific directions about the type of writing to be done, they leave lots of room for imagination. By using your imagination, you can discover fresh and exciting ideas that are distinctly yours. How can you come up with those bright ideas? Below are some techniques that can help you tap your creative powers. They can help you at the prewriting stage and any time you need to generate new ideas. You might use them to come up with a topic for a research paper, an essay, or a short story. You might use them to focus a topic or to generate ideas about a topic you've already chosen. Techniques such as outlining and clustering are also useful for organizing ideas. Try each of the techniques, and eventually you'll find the ones that work best for you for a particular purpose.

Free Writing. Have you ever been given a writing assignment and found that you had no idea what to write? Free writing is an activity for getting started—for coming up with ideas to write about. To free write, write anything that comes to mind, no matter how far off the topic it seems. At first it may seem silly, but eventually your mind will start associating ideas. Soon you will be writing complete thoughts about the topic.

Suppose you were asked to write about winter. How to begin? Start writing. Put down the first thought that comes to mind and let ideas begin to flow. You might come up with something like this:

> I don't know what to write. Winter. What can I say that hasn't already been said about winter? It's cold, there's lots of snow . . . well, not in all places I guess. Actually when it's cold here, it's warm on the other side of the world. Do they call that winter then, or summer . . . ?

Can you see how you might go from thoughts that are totally off the track to thoughts that are intriguing? When you have finished, look at all the ideas you've written down. Perhaps there are whole sentences or paragraphs that can go into your story or essay. This exercise will have gotten you started.

Brainstorming. This also is an activity to generate ideas. It can be done alone or in a group. When brainstorming, you want to come up with as many ideas as possible. Each idea will spur a new idea. As you or others in a brainstorming group think of ideas, write them down. After you have come up with all the ideas you can, select several to develop for the assignment.

Clustering. This technique can be useful both to generate ideas and to organize them. In fact, you actually do both at the same time, for as you jot down ideas, you "cluster" the ones that go together.

Begin by putting your main idea—your focused topic—in the center of the page and circling it. As you think of ideas associated with the main idea, write them nearby, circle them, and connect them with a line to the main idea. Then, as you think of ideas related to each of those *subtopics*, attach the ideas to the word they relate to. You can take this process as far as you like. The farther you branch out, the more detailed you get. When you get to the point where you're ready to write your story or your essay, you can use such a diagram as a guide to grouping your ideas. A simple clustering diagram is shown below. The main idea is "symbols in a story."

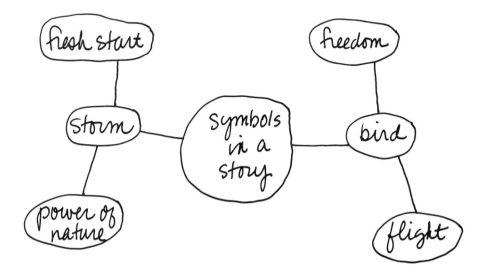

Using the Writing Process

Outlining. Outlining is usually thought of as an organizing tool, but it also provides a useful form in which to write down ideas as you think of them. It gives you a way to group ideas, just as clustering does. In addition, it helps you to organize those groups of ideas—to arrange them in the order in which you think you would like to write about them.

Start by writing down some main ideas that you want to include. Leave space after each one for listing related facts or thoughts—details— that you will want to include about the topic. Each idea you list will probably make you think of another idea. Look at the example below. Imagine that your assignment is to write a character sketch. You think you'd like to write about an old man. That's a main idea, so you write it down. One of the aspects of the man you want to talk about is his lifestyle. That, too, is a main idea, so you leave some space after your first idea and write it down. Okay, you ask yourself, what is the old man like? List each specific detail under the first main idea. Go on and do the same with lifestyle, and whatever other main ideas you may have.

Character Sketch

Old Man
about 80 years old
tall, thin, straight
athletic
friendly, outgoing
Man's Lifestyle
lives in his own apartment in the city
involved in theater
many friends of all ages

You can work back and forth in an outline, adding and deleting, until you're satisfied with the ideas that are there. Your last step will be to arrange the outline in the order in which you think you want to present the ideas in your writing. Then the outline becomes a kind of map for writing. Remember, though, that it's a loose map—you can rearrange, drop, and add ideas even as you are writing.

Outlining is also a good way of organizing the ideas you generate through brainstorming and free writing. It helps you place those ideas in some kind of order.

Stage 2: Writing

The second stage in the writing process is the writing itself. At this stage, you write a first draft of your paper or story, using the notes or outline that you developed in the prewriting stage as a guide. This is the stage at which you turn those loose ideas into sentences and paragraphs that work together.

Get Your Thoughts on Paper. When you begin writing, the most important thing to focus on is saying what you want to say—getting all your ideas down on paper in sentences and paragraphs. Some people find it easiest to write their first drafts without worrying if they have chosen exactly the right words and without checking on spelling. Just put a question mark next to anything you aren't sure of and check it later. You can even put a blank in a sentence if you can't think of the right word to put there. Fill it in when you revise.

As you are writing, you may discover that you sometimes have to go back and do some more thinking and planning. You may need to gather more information or think through an idea again. You may also do some rearranging of ideas.

Develop a Tone. In the writing stage, you need to begin to develop a tone—an attitude toward your subject. How do you want to *sound* to the reader? What impression do you want the reader to have toward the subject? Do you want to sound authoritative, amusing, sad, pleased?

You'll want to establish your tone right away—in the first paragraph. The first paragraph is important because it must grab your reader's interest and show where you are headed.

Organize Your Writing. As you write, you will, of course, be following the basic rules of the language. Sentences should express complete thoughts. They should follow one another in logical order. Each paragraph should focus on one main idea, and it should contain details that support that idea.

As you move from one paragraph to the next, use transition words and phrases to link your ideas. Clearly connect ideas and thoughts that go together so the reader can follow your story, argument, or explanation.

Stage 3: Revising

The third stage in the writing process is revising. This is the point at which you look for ways to polish your writing. Revising is more than just fixing a few errors. It can involve both major and minor changes.

Rethink Ideas and Organization

The first goal in revising is to check for clear, logical expression. Does what I have written make sense? Have I clearly said everything I am trying to say? Have I arranged my ideas in the best order?

Reread the entire draft to see if paragraphs and sentences follow in a logical order. You may find that putting paragraphs in a different order makes your points clearer. Remember that each paragraph is part of a whole, and it should relate to your topic. Sometimes you may write an excellent paragraph, only to discover that it has very little to do with the topic. No matter how good you think a sentence or a paragraph is, drop it if it doesn't belong.

As you read what you have written, you may also want to rewrite sentences and paragraphs, or even add new material. At this stage, you may also want to go back to your prewriting notes to see that you included everything you wanted to include.

Look at Your Language

After you have checked the ideas and organization, review the style and form in which you have written. Think about the language—the words and phrases you have used. Do they say precisely what you mean? Do they create strong images?

If you want your writing to be lively and interesting, write with strong verbs and nouns. They make strong writing. If you find yourself piling on the adjectives and adverbs, you'll know that you're struggling to support weak verbs and nouns. What is a strong verb or noun? It is one that is precise, active, fresh. It paints a clear picture in the mind.

Use Strong Verbs. Some verbs, for instance, are tired, overused, dull. The verb *to be*, for example, is about the weakest verb in the language. It doesn't *do* anything. So look at the sentences in which you use the verbs *is, are, am, was, have been,* etc. Are there action words that you can use instead? Instead of saying "Sam was happy," might you describe an action that *shows* that Sam was happy? "Sam smiled shyly and nodded his head," "Sam beamed," "Sam grinned," "Sam jumped into the air, arms raised above his head, and shouted, YES!"

Use Precise Nouns. Your nouns too should be precise. Whenever possible, create a strong image for the reader. The word *thing,* for instance, is imprecise and overused. What kind of image does it create in your mind? None. Search for the word that *tells.* If you are describing a street scene, for instance, instead of saying that there is a building on the corner, can you tell what kind of building it is? Is it a bank? A three-story Victorian house? A gothic cathedral? An open-air vegetable market? Draw clear pictures with your nouns.

Don't Overuse Adjectives and Adverbs. Adjectives and adverbs have their place, but try not to overdo them. When you do find yourself in need of an adjective, choose one that creates a strong image. Avoid those that are overused and don't really describe. *Beautiful* and *nice*, for instance, are overused adjectives.

Toss Out Unnecessary Words. Have you used more words than you need to say something? This is known as being redundant. Saying that someone is "bright and intelligent," for instance, is redundant because the adjectives are synonyms. Use one or the other. Another example is the phrase "crucially important." Why not just say "crucial"?

As you examine your language, throw out any words that don't serve a purpose—that don't give information, paint a clear picture, create atmosphere. By taking out unnecessary words, you will have "tight writing"—writing that moves along.

Check the Structure and Rhythm of Your Sentences. Read your work out loud and listen to the rhythm and sounds of the language. Do the sentences all sound the same? If they do, can you vary the structure of your sentences—making some simple, some complex, some long, some short? Correct any sentence fragments, and divide run-on sentences into two or more sentences.

After you've gone through that kind of thinking a few times at the revision stage, you'll find yourself automatically choosing livelier, clearer language as you write. You'll become a better writer. That, too, is a process.

Check for Errors

The final step in the revising process is the all-important "housekeeping" review—checking for correct spelling, grammar, and punctuation, and for readable handwriting. You don't, of course, have to wait until the end of the writing process to pay attention to those details. But before you write your final draft, check carefully for errors in those areas.

Checklist for the Writing Process

✓ What is my topic? Is it focused enough? Should I broaden or narrow it?

✓ What do I want to say about the topic? What are my thoughts, feelings, and ideas about it?

✓ Which prewriting activity or activities would most help me to gather ideas?

✓ Do I need to do some research? Some reading? Consult outside sources? What other materials, if any, do I need?

✓ What is the main point or idea that I want to communicate? What ideas are secondary? Which of those ideas are most important?

✓ What details will I include to support and expand on the main ideas?

✓ Should I include examples or anecdotes?

✓ How will I organize my ideas?

✓ What is my purpose for writing? Do I want to entertain? Inform? Explain? Persuade? Perhaps a combination?

✓ Who is my audience?

✓ What kind of language will I use? Will I be formal, informal, or casual? Will I use dialogue? Will I speak directly to the reader?

✓ What tone do I want to take—what feeling do I want to give the reader about the subject? How can I sustain that tone throughout my writing?

✓ How can I effectively begin my first paragraph? Should I use a question? A startling or unusual fact? An amazing statistic? Should I begin with an action or a description? Perhaps a piece of dialogue?

✓ How will I end? If writing nonfiction, should I summarize what I have already said, or should I offer a new thought or argument as my conclusion?

- ✓ Have I developed my ideas in the best order possible? Should I move some paragraphs around?

- ✓ Have I covered my topic adequately? Does the writing fulfill its purpose and get the main point across to my audience?

- ✓ Do I need to rewrite parts? Perhaps some ideas need to be clarified or explained further. Perhaps I could write a better description or account of an event?

- ✓ Do I want to add anything?

- ✓ Are there any unnecessary ideas or details that should be deleted?

- ✓ Is each paragraph well developed—are the facts and ideas presented in a good order?

- ✓ Do all the sentences in each paragraph relate to one idea?

- ✓ Are the ideas between sentences and between paragraphs connected with transition words and phrases that make the connections clear?

- ✓ Is the writing vivid? Have I used active, precise, colorful words that create strong images?

- ✓ Does the final paragraph provide a good ending?

- ✓ Are the sentences well constructed? Are there any run-ons or sentence fragments that need fixing? Do I vary the kinds of sentences—some long, some short, some active, some passive?

- ✓ Is the grammar correct?

- ✓ Are all the words spelled correctly?

- ✓ Is all the punctuation correct?

- ✓ Is the final draft clean and legible?

- ✓ Have I read the final draft over one last time to check for any errors that may have crept in as I was copying?

Glossary of Literary Terms

This glossary includes definitions for all the important literary terms introduced in this book. The first time they are defined and discussed in the text, the terms are underlined. Following each term in the glossary is a page reference (in parentheses) that tells the page on which the term is introduced.

Many terms are discussed in more than one chapter, especially as they apply to various poems. This glossary provides the fullest definition of each term. Boldfaced words within the definitions are other terms that appear in the glossary.

alliteration (page 63) the close repetition of the same first sounds in words, usually consonant sounds, at the beginnings of words. An example of alliteration in "The Raven," by Edgar Allan Poe, is: "Once upon a midnight dreary, while I pondered weak and weary." Poets use alliteration to add emphasis to an idea or to certain words, or to heighten the mood of a line or a stanza. Although alliteration usually occurs at the beginnings of words, it can also occur within words.

apostrophe (page 124) the method of addressing a thing or an absent person as though that thing or person is present.

assonance (page 64) the repetition of similar vowel sounds within words to emphasize certain sounds and add a musical quality. An example of assonance in "The Raven," by Edgar Allan Poe, occurs in the following line: "For the rare and radiant maiden whom the angels name Lenore."

ballad (page 172) a song that tells a simple story. Many ballads have been passed from generation to generation by word of mouth before being written down. Most ballads are written in four-line stanzas. Many ballads contain **epithets** and a **refrain.**

blank verse (page 43) an unrhymed poem that is written in **iambic pentameter.**

characters (page 20) the people, animals, things, or even machines that carry out the action of a story or a poem.

climax (page 21) the most dramatic moment of the **plot**; the point of highest tension and greatest interest for the reader. The climax is usually the turning point of the story or poem.

concrete language (page 84) words that describe things that the reader knows and understands with his or her senses. Concrete language describes something that actually exists and can be seen or touched in the reader's mind. *See* **image** and **imagery.**

connotation (page 86) the emotion that a word arouses or the meanings it suggests beyond its **denotation,** or dictionary meaning.

consonance (page 64) occurs in words where the consonant sounds stay the same but the vowel sounds are different as in pitter, patter and spin, spun.

denotation (page 85) the dictionary meaning of a word.

dialect (page 94) the special words, expressions, and pronunciations that are unique to people of a certain group or of a particular region.

dialogue (page 180) the actual conversation between the characters.

end rhyme (page 61) the repetition of syllable sounds that occurs at the ends of lines of poetry. *See* **rhyme scheme.**

epithet (page 181) a descriptive word or phrase that expresses a quality or characteristic of an object or a person. An epithet is often used in place of the name of a person or thing. The epithet "Lion-Hearted" is commonly used for Richard I of England, who is referred to as Richard the Lion-Hearted.

extended metaphor (page 123) a special kind of **metaphor** that involves the entire poem. The shorter metaphors within the poem contribute directly to the main metaphor. The purpose of an extended metaphor is to create a strong, lasting image.

eye rhyme (page 89) the use of words that appear to rhyme, but do not, as if they rhymed. An example of eye rhyme is the words *maid* and *said.*

feminine rhyme (page 62) rhyming words that consist of a stressed syllable followed by one or more unstressed syllables. A feminine rhyme in "The Raven," by Edgar Allan Poe, occurs with the words *napping* and *tapping.* Feminine rhymes can also be made from two or more words together, such as *made he, stayed he,* and *lady.*

figurative language (page 95) words and phrases used in unusual ways to create strong, vivid images, to focus attention on certain ideas, and to compare things that are basically different. When words or phrases are used figuratively, they have meanings other than their usual, or literal, meanings. *See* specific **figures of speech** such as **metaphor, personification,** and **simile.**

figure of speech (page 95) a word or phrase that creates a vivid image by contrasting unlike things. A figure of speech has meanings other than its ordinary meaning.

foot (page 19) the unit in which **meter** is counted. A foot consists of one stressed syllable and its one or more unstressed syllables. The number of feet in a line of poetry equals the number of stressed syllables. *See* **scanning** and **stress.**

free verse (page 43) a poem that does not have any fixed meter, rhyme, or line length. The rhythm may vary from line to line or within a line. The verse is called "free" because the poet is free to change the patterns or to use no pattern at all. Much twentieth-century poetry is written in free verse.

hyperbole (page 108) a figure of speech in which the truth is exaggerated in order to emphasize an idea or a feeling. "I've told you that a million times" is an example of hyperbole.

iamb (page 42) a foot that consists of one unstressed and one stressed syllable. *See* **meter** and **iambic pentameter.**

iambic pentameter (page 42) a five-foot line in which each foot is an **iamb.** In English poetry iambic pentameter is used more often than any other **meter.**

image (page 71) a word or phrase that creates a mental picture of something for the reader. Although most images are visual, an image can appeal to any of the other senses—sight, sound, taste, smell, and touch. Some images appeal to more than one sense at a time.

imagery (page 84) all the **images** that are created in a poem. *See* **specific image** and **concrete image.**

implicit metaphor (page 106) a special kind of **metaphor** in which one of the terms is not stated but suggested by the context. "The children flocked to the ice cream stand" is an example of an implicit metaphor in which the children are indirectly compared to sheep by the word *flocked.*

internal rhyme (page 62) the kind of rhyme that occurs when a word within a line rhymes with another word in that line. *See* **feminine rhyme** and **masculine rhyme.**

irony (page 183) a contrast between what is said and what is meant. People use irony when they say one thing but mean the opposite. "I love to be told that I'm wrong all the time" is an example of verbal irony in which the speaker means the opposite of what he or she is saying.

lyric poem (page 87) a poem that has a single speaker and expresses a deeply felt thought or emotion. The speaker does not have a specific audience; that is, the speaker seems to be addressing himself or herself. A **sonnet** is a type of lyric poem.

masculine rhyme (page 62) rhyming words of one stressed syllable. An example of masculine rhyme in "The Raven," by Edgar Allan Poe, occurs with the words *lore* and *door*.

metaphor (page 41) an imaginative implied comparison between two unlike things. A metaphor is a comparison that suggests one thing *is* another. The purpose of a metaphor is to give the reader an unusual way of looking at one of the things. *See* **figurative language.**

meter (page 19) the regular pattern of stressed and unstressed syllables in a line of poetry. Meter is counted in feet. The most common meter in English poetry is **iambic pentameter.** *See* **foot** and **stress.**

monologue (page 147) the situation in a poem in which there is only one speaker. In a monologue the speaker may be addressing one or more people.

mood (page 41) the general feeling or atmosphere created in a poem.

narrative poetry (page 6) poetry that tells a story. The story may be true or it may be imagined, as in "The Cremation of Sam McGee" by Robert Service.

onomatopoeia (page 65) the use of words whose sounds imitate, echo, or suggest their meanings. Examples of onomatopoeia are the words *crash, buzz*, and *hiss*. Poets use onomatopoeia to add humor, to reinforce the meaning of a line, or to create an image.

pentameter (page 42) a five-foot line. *See* **meter.**

persona (page 149) the voice that the poet creates for the **speaker.** The persona has a character.

personification (page 126) a figure of speech in which an animal, an object, or an idea is given human qualities. Poets often use personification to describe abstract ideas such as freedom, truth, and beauty. *See* **figurative language.**

plot (page 21) the sequence of events in a story or narrative poem.

Glossary of Literary Terms

poetry (page 15) a type of literature in which the rhythm, sound, and meaning of language are arranged to create powerful images and feelings. Poetry is arranged in lines with a regular rhythm and sometimes a pattern of rhyme and is characterized by compactness of language and the use of imagery and figurative language. Poems vary greatly, however, and some kinds of poetry do not have a regular rhythm or rhyme. *See* **blank verse** and **free verse.**

prose (page 15) the ordinary form of written or spoken language, without any rhyme or regular rhythm. It is the language of our everyday activities, as well as the language of novels, short stories, essays, and many plays.

pun (page 245) a humorous play on words in which the words sound alike but have different meanings.

quatrain (page 107) a four-line **stanza,** and a very common form in English poetry.

refrain (page 181) one or more lines that are repeated regularly throughout a poem. A refrain is often found in a **ballad.**

rhetorical question (page 104) a question asked only for dramatic effect and not to seek an answer.

rhyme (page 60) the repetition of the same or similar stressed sound or sounds *(beat, heat, seat)*. Rhyme is often related to meaning because it brings two or more words together. *See* **end rhyme, feminine rhyme, internal rhyme, masculine rhyme,** and **rhyme scheme.**

rhyme scheme (page 61) the pattern of end rhyme in a poem. A poem has a rhyme scheme when the words at the ends of two or more lines rhyme. Rhyme scheme adds to the musical sound of poetry and can affect the **mood** of a poem. The rhyme scheme of a poem can be shown by assigning a different letter of the alphabet to each different line-end sound in a stanza. Lines that rhyme are given the same letter. For example, if the first and second lines have one rhyme and the third and fourth lines have another, the rhyme scheme would be *aabb.*

rhythm (page 18) the pattern of stressed and unstressed syllables in a poem. Through rhythm, a poet can highlight the musical quality of language. Rhythm can serve other purposes, such as emphasizing ideas or making actions more vivid. The standard way of showing the rhythm of a poem is by using symbols: / for a stressed syllable, and ∪ for an unstressed syllable.

scanning (page 19) counting the feet, or number and arrangement of stressed and unstressed syllables in a line to determine the **meter.** *See* **foot** and **stress.**

setting (page 20) the time and place of the action of a story or narrative poem.

simile (page 103) a direct comparison between two unlike things that are connected by *like, as,* or *resembles* or the verb *appears* or *seems.* The purpose of a simile is to give the reader a vivid new way of looking at one of the things. *See* **figurative language.**

sonnet (page 88) a fourteen-line **lyric poem** with a fixed pattern of rhythm and meter. The lines are usually in **iambic pentameter.** An Italian sonnet has two parts: an eight-line part in which the poet discusses his or her thoughts about an experience, and a six-line part in which the poet responds to or comments on the experience.

speaker (page 6) the voice that talks in a poem. The speaker may or may not be the poet. The speaker may be a character that the poet has created and may even be an animal or an object. *See* **persona.**

stanza (page 17) a group of lines that forms a section of a poem. Each stanza often has the same rhyme pattern.

stress (page 18) words or syllables that receive greater accent, or emphasis, than others. Stress gives a word or syllable greater force or prominence in a line of poetry.

structure (page 27) the poet's arrangement or overall design of the work. In poetry structure refers to the way the words and lines are arranged to produce a particular effect.

suspense (page 59) the interest, excitement, and anticipation that a reader feels about what will happen in the poem or story.

symbol (page 39) a person, a place, or an object that stands for something other or more important than itself.

theme (page 89) the underlying message of a piece of writing.

tone (page 105) a writer's attitude toward his or her subject, audience, or self.